Beyond the Floathouse

Gunhild's Granddaughter

by Myrtle Siebert

Recording lives of early pioneer residents along
the remote waterways of the BC Coast

Myrtle Rae Farley Siebert

ISBN: 978-0-9880709-1-2

Editors: Suzanne Schrader, Esther Hart, and Linda Clement

Front cover: Forberg floathouse. Myrtle and Grandmother Gunhild.
Photos by Hazel Forberg
Back cover: Port Neville dock. 2002. Photo by Myrtle Siebert.
All photos inside of the book courtesy of Myrtle's family

Cover design by Iryna Spica
Typeset in *Haarlemmer* with *Scotch Roman* display at SpicaBookDesign

Printed in Canada

for my children,
Norma and Eric Siebert and Linda Ackermann
and grandchildren,
Tait, Tessa, Tori Ackermann

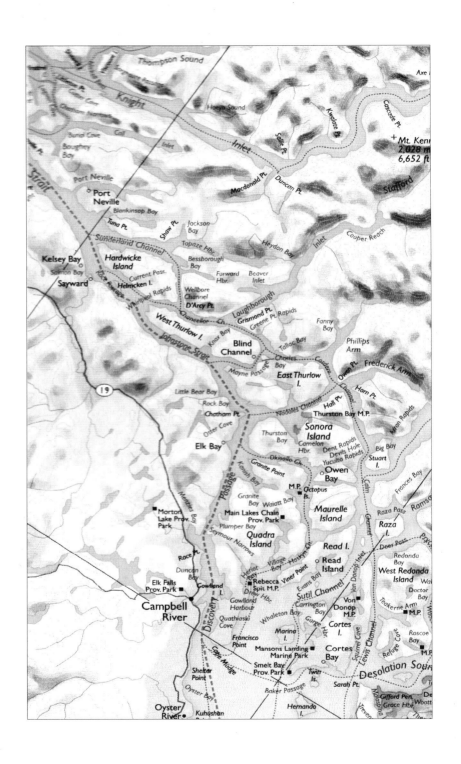

Table of Contents

Gunhild Gunnulfson and Einar Einarson.

1.
Arrivals

I n May of 1893, a twenty-one–year-old Norwegian, Einar Einarson Forberg, disembarked from the ship, *Venetia*, in New York Harbour and was processed by immigration officials at Ellis Island. He and his twenty-three-year-old travelling partner, Ole Johnsen, whose family owned an adjacent farm in Bo, Telemark, were bound for Michigan. I learned this when I found both names in the ship's passenger records, after I had found the farms on a map of Norway.

Einar was the man I knew all my life as Andy Forberg, my grandfather. Upon leaving the ship, he had done as many of his countrymen had done: adopted a permanent family name by using the name of the family farm, Forberg, which means "before, or in front of, the rock or cliff." I have seen both the farm and the rock and they are aptly named.

In 1898, with excitement running high about news of the Klondike Gold Rush, Andy and Ole left the forests of Michigan where they had been working, and set out for Vancouver, Canada. Arriving at the coast they learned that there was a new restriction placed on gold seekers: anyone going to the gold fields was required to have enough money for "grubstake and gear," approximately $500.

As partners, Andy and Ole had saved only enough funds for one of them to go. Their solution was to flip a coin. Andy lost. Had he won, I might have been born in the United States, with a completely different story to tell. After his time in the gold fields, Ole settled in Wrangell, Alaska. When I travelled there to do research, I learned he had established a hardware store that, until it closed, had been well known by my friends living in the area. Details of this story were written in my book, *from Fjord to Floathouse, one family's journey from the farmlands of Norway to the coast of British Columbia.*

Having lost the flip of a coin, Andy remained behind and set out to carve a livelihood from the remote forests of British Columbia. I am his granddaughter and this is my story.

I arrived on the Port Neville scene early in August of 1938, a babe in arms on board *MV Chelosin*. It was the same ship my parents had boarded in Jackson Bay for their honeymoon the year before. I can imagine the reception we had at the Port Neville dock. Postmistress Karen Hansen, who had no children of her own, was there to welcome a new soul to the Port Neville community with her mother, surrounded by children in a range of ages who would all need to look. There, a new baby, clothed in tenderly knitted matching jacket, charming hat tied under the chin and booties, wrapped in a crocheted shawl (I have it carefully folded away) with a corner of it tossed over mom's shoulder. My mother, Hazel Mae (Fearing) Forberg, wore a smart suit, heeled pumps and fashionable cloche hat over freshly-permed short hair; I have the photograph.

The boat trip always took two days, with stops at each port to deliver supplies and pick up and deliver residents' mail. Think how difficult it was to manage a newborn alone, take meals in the formal dining room with mostly men and only a few women, all returning to camp after doctor or dentist visits or, in the case of some, recovering from a booze bender. Imagine how badly she just wanted to get home by the time she arrived at the dock. But wait, Hazel and her husband Buster would want to also take home the mail that Karen had begun to sort, so a welcome cup of tea in the Hansen home was offered.

Union Steamship leaving Vancouver on the way North.

Given the dependability of stops by the Union Steamship boat, an expectant mother needed to plan her exodus to Vancouver in good time for delivery of the baby. For a first baby she might allow more than a month before the due date, but in any case she allowed at least a month. My Uncle Ingolf, Dad's younger brother, was born in February of a particularly cold winter when Loughborough Inlet, where the Senior Forbergs were living, had frozen over. Fortunately his mother, my Grandmother Gunhild, had the good sense to accept an invitation to bring her other two children and spend Christmas in Jackson Bay. From there she could be certain of getting away when the Union Steamship arrived on its southern route to Vancouver. Midwives were not available, and even if they had been, getting one to the home where she was needed could risk loss of the father and the midwife in stormy seas.

My mother had traveled to Vancouver at least a month earlier and delivered me in Vancouver General Hospital. Whenever we went to Vancouver in later years, the Golinski home was where we stayed, as mom had while waiting for

labour to begin. The daughters had been Mom's school chums, and we could always depend on that family's hospitality. Grandma Golinski and her warm kitchen were central to many of our happy memories of exploring parts of that unfamiliar city and her generously endowed body was lovingly embraced by all who came – adults and babies alike.

All of the Hansens who were at home on the day of my arrival were there at the dock with my father to welcome us. The Hansen family lived in a big log house on the only cultivated land in the surrounding area. Their farm property produced food for the family and gave their children space to explore and to play. Olaf did a bit of hand logging and beach combing too, but it was the Port Neville Post Office that gave them a dependable income.

Olaf Hansen's father, Hans Hansen, had been one of the first pioneers to settle in Port Neville. He had come from Norway in 1877, and had originally worked at Hastings Mill in Vancouver, much as my grandfather did 20 years later. By stages he had made his way up the coast, by sailing and rowing, eventually landing at Port Neville in 1891. When the Post Office, an institution that was such an integral part of all of our lives, began operation in Port Neville in November of 1895, Hans Hansen became its first Postmaster. When she arrived from Norway in 1903, Mrs. Hansen was sworn in as Assistant Postmistress.

The Hansen's massive log structure at the end of the government dock housed the Post Office in front and included a small general store. Although the front of the building was where business took place, on Boat Day some of us were invited into the Hansen family living quarters at the back of the building. A daughter, Lilly Hansen, remembered, "On Boat Day several dozen people might stay for supper, or at least sit down for a cup of coffee while the mail was being sorted."

When I was older, and allowed to go with my dad for Boat Day, I delighted in having a rare opportunity to play with other children in their back yard. Ole Hansen, son of Olaf, was my age, but as the only boy among sisters he was more likely to be around the men and their boats. If the steamboat happened to come late that day, I would welcome a longer time to visit before returning to camp. This was the place people congregated to share the news, both good and bad, and make brief contact with neighbours of the scattered community of surrounding area residents who gave Port Neville as their return address. The Post Office was a single, crucial uniting element.

Unmarried Grandpa Andy Forberg's 'camp' about 1907-08.

Grandpa Andy worked first at the Hastings Mill on the south shore of Vancouver's harbour. Wages then were approximately a dollar a day. New Westminster was the earliest residential community in the area, and for years after his arrival in Canada he and his family regularly visited friends who had settled there. Andy's life evolved as a coastal hand logger, which at the time meant that he cut the trees with hand saw and axe and brought them down to the ocean using only ingenuity with a *peavey*, a *jack* and brute strength.

He made his way northward in his rowboat, working intermittently at each stop. For a time he worked at Powell River, then moved on up Johnstone Strait, and finally into several of the coastal indentions including Loughborough Inlet, Sunderland Channel and Topaz Harbour. See map on an opening page.

After ten years of living alone, or with a work partner, he went back to Norway and returned with a thirty-year-old woman to be his wife. My mother told me Gunhild Gunnulfson was Andy's childhood friend, but when I did family history research

I discovered she was also his first cousin. Gunhild Gunnulfson and Einar Einarson Forberg were my father's parents.

My maternal grandparents, the Fearings – Bill Fearing, originally from Hingham Massachusetts, and Katie Clooten, born in Belgium – made their way from Alberta to Vancouver. There my Fearing grandfather formed a partnership with a man named Sinclair. They built homes in Vancouver's Shaughnessy area and, assisted by his sons, built two others on Duff Street where they lived. His wife Katie kept goats and sold milk to the Shaughnessy Hospital.

Bill and Katie Fearing in 1961.

It was Grandpa Bill Fearing's dream to be away from what he considered an unhealthy city life and to "live off the land." In answer to a newspaper ad, they eventually traded the Vancouver home for a 140-acre partly-wooded property in Jackson Bay, near Topaz Harbour. Included in the transaction were a log house and a boat, essential for transportation. As boat trips went, Jackson Bay was considered a short ride from Port Neville.

The entire Fearing family moved and took up residency as farmers in the rustic log home and re-established their life on a farm. Grandpa Bill did some hand logging, like most men who lived on the coast, and my grandmother Katie sold garden produce and eggs, and ran the post office that was on their property.

Both of my grandparent families had survived the deprivation of World War I and the Great Depression of the 30s without major losses, primarily by living off the land. Although the outside world had changed a great deal by 1938, when I was born in Vancouver and brought to live in Port Neville, the water-constrained area in which my parents met and married remained much as it had been for nearly fifty years.

British Columbia is located in Canada, on the western edge of the North American continent above the 49th parallel. Its northern rocky coastline is frequently indented with winding inlets and islands reminiscent of the fjords of my grandfather's Norwegian homeland. Vancouver Island is a long, narrow land mass about the same size as the Netherlands; it drapes itself in front of smaller islands and numerous inlets, and partially protects the area from the full force of the wildest Pacific storms.

When Andy Forberg began moving northward, away from his first job in what we now refer to as the Vancouver area, Port Neville, with a post office at the mouth of the inlet, was the northernmost stop for the steamboat plying the Inside Passage. The approximately eight-mile-long Port Neville inlet is a classic example of British Columbia's northern coast, with forests and heavy undergrowth extending right down to the rocky beaches, making penetration inland very difficult.

As in all underdeveloped areas, some of the earliest residents were unmarried men, or men whose wives remained elsewhere until a place could be made ready for them. They tended to be independent-minded and most of them had made their way north up the coastline from Vancouver as my grandfather had done. Many were recent immigrants; it was employment that had originally brought these people to this remote area. In a few instances they were the second generation of coastal families. Most of the men were hand loggers who worked alone, or formed working partnerships with other men. A few relied on beach combing, and those who owned fishing boats might choose to go out with the salmon fleet for a few months during the summer fishing season.

At the oceanside location, where the floathouses were tied, there were no roads and there still are not; there was no electricity, and as of this writing, there still is not. There was no land phone, and there still is not. During the years we lived on the coast there was not even a radio phone. Residents listened to battery-powered radios for news in the evening, when the transmission signal was clearest, or read the two-week-old weekend *Star Weekly*. My grandparents also received months-old papers and journals mailed to them from Norway. Communication and transportation by water was the only choice. Even in an emergency, there was certainly no way anyone could call for help from a float plane. That meant owning a boat was essential, and letter writing was fundamental for keeping in touch.

Each of my four grandparents had come to Canada as immigrants and made this coast their chosen home. It may not have been what they expected, but they prospered, and my three children are the ultimate beneficiaries.

The harness allowed a child's freedom to move.

2.
Our Floathouse Home

W ithout any cleared land along Port Neville inlet, the rest of the families lived much as we did. Houses were small to facilitate easier heating. Each one sat on *skids*, two logs braced together much like an overgrown sled. The house on its skids was positioned on high-floating logs tied together with cable to form a float. This (a small house, or cabin, secured on logs) is what we called a *floathouse*. When the float's logs became waterlogged they could be replaced, or in some future circumstance, the house itself pulled up on solid land, the way ours was some years later at Rock Bay.

Wood construction for houses was the norm, and roofs were tarpaper or hand split cedar shakes. Insulation didn't exist, so winter winds blowing between the skids cooled the floors and left residents shivering when they crept from bed. A wood-fired cook stove heated our house; it had an attached reservoir to heat water for sponge baths and clothes washing but it took some time for the hot firebox next to it to heat the volume of cold water it contained.

As I think of what it was like to wake up in that draughty house, I appreciate more than ever my father's morning routine. He was always the first one up, and using several pieces of dry kindling he would scratch together the live embers in the cook stove. Provided he had banked it at bedtime with large blocks, or bark, there would be a few sparks, or at least the firebox was still hot, and he could encourage flames from a lit match put to a bit of paper.

Our floating camp buildings.

Once he had a serious flame burning, that could ignite regular firewood, it seemed only a short time before the fire was crackling again. Soon thereafter mom had the kettle boiling on the stove and porridge cooking for us. She would call out to us from the kitchen, "Time to get up now girls. Wash your face and get dressed, porridge is nearly ready."

I dreaded the feeling of splashing cold water from the wash bowl on my face, but that was the expected routine. We did have a tiny washroom with a sink and cold running water to it where morning absolutions could be performed and dad could shave at the end of his work day. The space also held a toilet-height wood box with a seat that we used for urination—liquid ran through to the beach. For solid waste we used a separate outhouse building that sat on the float beside the woodshed.

Stoves required regular and frequent replenishment of chopped wood, as did an auxiliary heater if there was one. Heaters were welcome on the stormiest days, but they needed to be fed too. Our airtight heater, an oval metal shape, sat proudly in the corner of the front room ready to be called into service on the coldest winter days or for special occasions when we had guests.

From the time I was strong enough to carry three or four sticks of wood, it was my chore to keep the wood box behind the cook stove filled. When dad came home from work he chopped the cedar kindling for the next day and helped me top up the wood box. Then, when I was a bit older, he presented me with a safer single-bit axe, much like one campers keep with their outdoor gear, and taught me how to chop kindling. Five years younger than me, my sister was old enough and strong enough by then to take over the wood box-filling chore.

More modern homes had oil cook stoves and heaters that required no stoking, but those had disadvantages, especially if the oil barge came late or was delayed by storms. A heavy wind blowing a downdraft could spread a black sooty mess on everything. When this happened to our new oil stove some years later, my mother despaired of ever having a clean kitchen again, as she wiped determinedly all the dirtied surfaces. It didn't help much, I'm sure, that both my parents and most of their friends were cigarette smokers.

Good housekeeping meant a clean chimney and mom reminded my father to clean ours regularly. They chose a calm day when she could let the fire go out before he began banging on the black metal chimney pipe with a smooth piece of firewood. So armed, he would climb an outside ladder to the roof and crawl the short distance to the chimney where he banged it, then climbed down, and up another ladder inside the house and up to the attic. Each time he banged we heard the thumps and occasionally the sound of a dislodged chunk of encrusted soot dropping to the firebox. Next was removal of the warm ashes to a red metal bucket borrowed from the fire gear that the government required all logging companies to keep. He was able to relight the fire in time for our next meal. On those days, usually a Sunday because dad was home, I remember mom serving pancakes and bacon, or clam chowder made in the morning and set aside to reheat when the cleaning job was finished.

The coastal people were essentially nomadic, with floating homes movable from bay to bay as new opportunities were presented. Every family needed a boat of some sort. When new timber sales were identified by government and made available to individuals and companies, those hand loggers who required more timber were able to bid. Thus the moving process for successful bidders began again. The camp, with its floating houses and equipment rafts, needed to be towed to the new location. When a move was decided upon, one of the Forberg men would write to, or speak in person to, a tug company employee and arrange for a more powerful boat, or tug, to be on hand.

Forberg float-camp being moved.

Gunhild's Granddaughter

When it was ready for the move, our camp of assorted-sized floats, all joined together by heavy cables, was a tandem tow. Nano and Grandpa Forberg's float was the largest. On it was their dark green shake house, Uncle Ingolf's bunkhouse and their outhouse. On our float was the creamy yellow shake-covered house with its matching woodshed and outhouse, all enclosed by a gated chicken wire fence to keep the children safe from going overboard.

A separate raft was loaded with hand logging equipment: blocks, tackle, peaveys, jacks, spring boards, pike poles, fire-fighting gear and my grandfather's forge, with a lean-to that protected it from rain as he worked. Most important of all for the success of Forberg Logging was the A-frame float with its steam powered donkey and cable drums. In my child's eyes the donkey was an ugly, grease-encrusted black thing that growled and belched smoke and steam while straining to pull a log. Of course, drums of fuel for all powered equipment needed space on one of the floats.

A successful move required choosing the right placement for the floathouses. The place chosen to tie a floathouse needed to have a creek or river nearby for a year-round water supply. At low tide the floor of the house sloped proportionally to the slope of the beach, so for the best living conditions my family tried to locate their floathouses on a wide, flat beach. If the floathouses were pushed into place on a semi-yearly maximum high tide, then only in the worst storms would it move and rock when floating on a high tide.

Much of the shoreline was rocky, or had steep cliffs, so if a family could not find a suitable place sufficiently near to work, then the float was secured to the bluff, and remained permanently floating. When a strong wind blew up, living in a floathouse in that position was like being on an unseaworthy

Our Floathouse Home   15

cruise ship. Fortunately, we were never tied in that way but I visited some families who were.

Once in place, our floathouses were secured to shore by heavy cables wound around large, live trees. A wide sturdy log served as a *stiff-leg,* and provided us with stable way to walk on to the beach. When the floats were secured to land the men hauled a length of rubber hose for each house up the creek, far enough away so the intake would not to be affected by tidal salt water. The other end was connected to the kitchen taps — this was our water supply system.

Heavy rain could provide silty, brown water that we allowed to settle in a bucket before we drank it or used it for cooking. I can remember my mother despairing of ever having her whites white again. That's when Mrs. Stewarts Bluing, Whitening Whites Safely since 1883, came to the rescue. When I think of what mom, and all the other women of those times, had to endure to make our clothes clean I shudder. First they scooped hot water from the wood stove boiler to an aluminum washtub (the same round one we all used to bath in on Saturday night), then scrubbed the clothes by hand using laundry bar soap on a glass scrubbing board. They had to wring everything by hand and then rinse and wring again, after which they hung the wet, often heavy, garments on a clothes line strung from their house to a tree on shore. That line, with its pulleys, was just one more thing to re-attach after every move.

For very wet or stormy days, we had a wood rail rack for drying clothes indoors. When mom had the lighter items in place the rack could be drawn up to the kitchen ceiling, leaving our hot house moist and steamy. In later years, a partly enclosed covered porch was added to one whole side of the house which held additional clotheslines strung the entire length.

Dealing with cloth diapers, other baby clothing and women's personal items to most of us seems bad enough, but just imagine washing sweat-encrusted Stanfield wool underwear (long johns and long-sleeved shirts) along with smelly work socks and greasy, muddy, or dusty, heavy work pants. My sister tells of the day mom's gas-motorized washing machine with hand wringers was delivered to our float. Dad had taken me to school in Rock Bay that day so I didn't see the event but it must have been quite a performance. Dad arrived home in time to help position the scow, with a washing machine on board, alongside our float and help the men make the transfer across the space of water between the two. After ten years of hand washing and hand wringing, for my mother it was truly a red letter day.

Waste systems were simple. Kitchen refuse went over the side of the float for the sea birds to fight over. Outhouses on a float were not as rank-smelling as those on a farm because with every tidal change the evidence washed away. A *thunder pot* lived under every bed for nighttime emergencies.

Preparation of food for the family, or a small family-based logging crew, was the accepted role of women, much as the same role was undertaken by prairie farm women. But women who lived in a floathouse weren't able to rely on their garden to provide vegetables, nor were chickens or cows available to provide eggs and milk. My Fearing grandmother, whom I called Little Nano, at least had access to fresh farm produce from which to prepare her meals and could can some for winter use.

My mother and both of my grandmothers assumed their role of wife, mother and cook, as an important and challenging career. For a part of my life I did the same, but what a tremendous difference there was between my experience, of feeding our young family in a fully-electric kitchen, and that of my mother and grandmothers. Working with food has been a constant part of my life and became an important aspect of my professional career. It was during the first summer of my marriage, when I went to cook for dad and his brother at their beach-based work camp, that I faced the vicissitudes of a wood-fired cook stove. It was then that I fully appreciated the kitchen

Nano and me with buckets of abalone.

experiences of the mothers who went before me. Have you ever made bread? Have you baked bread in the oven of a wood-fired stove? For my foremothers, bread-making was a chore to be done at least every other day.

Provisioning the kitchen was an ongoing challenge for any Port Neville homemaker, requiring resourcefulness, patience and strength. Anything that could not be caught, picked, or shot came on The Union Steamship vessel when it called at the Port Neville government dock every two weeks. The supplies it brought had been ordered from Vancouver by outgoing mail on the ship's previous visit. We had no refrigeration, or even an ice box, so salad foods were unknown in our kitchen. What most homes had was a fine wire-mesh enclosed cooler; ours was attached to the ocean side of the house overhanging the water where cooling breezes could move between the smooth slats of its shelves. Here was where we kept meat, butter, cheese and an opened can of milk and occasionally stored cabbage for a few days. I was first introduced to lettuce at Nano Fearing's farmhouse because anything as delicate as lettuce would not have survived a week on board a Union Steamship vessel.

Vegetables, some fruits, and milk all came to us canned, and they arrived in case lots. Onions, turnips, parsnips, potatoes and carrots would keep for a while, and they came in gunnysacks. Flour, oatmeal, rice and sugar came in bulk too—twenty pound fabric bags—and even the fabric used for those bags was valuable. We washed, bleached and used it to make tablecloths and pillowcases. I learned to do embroidery on them. I still have some of the pillowslips made that way.

Floathouse life meant that fish and shellfish were readily available: clams, mussels, abalone, prawns and shrimp abounded. Wild game, including deer, grouse and duck were staple meats and easily obtained when one of the men had a day free during hunting season. My mother was an excellent shot, perfected while she was growing up with three competitive brothers. It was not unusual, then or in her later life, for her to be the family member to bring home venison for the table or a brace of grouse or ducks for a flavourful stew. The steady trolling motion needed for salmon fishing required more upper-body strength than most women had, but jigging for a cod could be done from a rowboat. Depending on the tide, one of mom's favourite afternoon exercises was rowing out to the kelp bed to catch a cod lurking there.

In the spring and summer months, when tides were low during daylight, digging for clams was a welcome outing for women, children and any available men. There were few restrictions on how many we could take at any one time, so a group of people working together could dig several bucketsful. When allowed to sit in ocean water for a few hours and fed oatmeal, the clams would clean themselves, excreting waste and sand in the process. If we collected enough, any extra clams could be canned for future use. A pressure canner was an important household implement used for preserving staples of salmon, clams, mussels, venison, and any other game meat that could be obtained.

Home decoration and maintenance, clothing for the family and care for children, all done in the face of inconvenience, scarcity, stormy weather and hard work, were also part of a women's role. This was the glory age of catalogues and much of what a family needed, including all that important gear for workmen—coats, hats, boots, rainwear, work pants—was shown, described and ordered from Eaton's and, later, Woodward's catalogue. Capable women sewed their own clothes, using either a pedal-powered or hand-cranked sewing machine. The fabric was chosen from the catalogue as were the needles, thread and trims. Many of us grew up wearing improperly sized shoes, or footwear that had been outgrown by others. Adult garments were re-cut and sewn into children's clothing.

My mother was thrifty and able to make something from virtually nothing, but there was one remake I remember as a complete failure. On that occasion she used my uncle's worn army uniform to re-cut and sew into a snowsuit for me. Mom was an excellent seamstress, and the suit looked quite respectable. She had turned the fabric inside out to camouflage its origins but that left a rough surface against my skin. I was a solidly built child with thick legs, and when the fabric rubbed between my heavy thighs I could scarcely bear to wear the suit, it was so itchy.

Remote coastal areas are challenging to this day because of the long, high-banked, inlets that make radio and telephone reception of every kind unreliable. At least today boats move more quickly and air travel is available. With a reduced population, the economic reality of providing costly services to residents on the mainland coast of British Columbia has lessened focus on the needs of people of that area.

A summer picnic with the Forbergs. Dad's Rae-Lee at anchor.

On board Dad's Lutie with the Fearing relatives.

As might be expected, people created their own recreation and amusements. A favourite pastime was to gather for the evening over cards or board games, followed by a decadent dessert baked by the hostess. It made for a pleasant evening, but because the men left for work at dawn it finished early. My mother loved a hike or berry-picking outing because it was land-based and a change from our daily surroundings. I remember the excellent fried chicken my grandmother Gunhild made to take on a picnic we held at "The Narrows" of Port Neville on a fine summer day when the Golinski sisters were visiting us. Sunday was the one day the men were free to take us by boat away from our beach location.

Saturday night was the only available "late night" for a dance, box social or whist drive. Dad taught me to dance very early, first by having me stand on his shoes as he moved across the floor, and then when I was tall enough, teaching me the steps as his six-foot-one, two-hundred-twenty-pound frame guided me through them. He had good sense of rhythm and was smooth and light on his feet. Under his guidance I learned the schottische, polka and the old time Swedish waltz. His all-time favourite was Blue Skirt Waltz; to hear it now brings tears to my eyes.

As for a spiritual life, individual men and women looked after that themselves and taught children as they saw fit. The Columbia Coast Mission boats traveled the coast delivering Bibles, hymn books and children's books of Bible stories, but their ability to conduct church services was limited by their irregular visits to far-flung communities and the cramped space aboard their ships. Ministers were called upon to conduct

Gunhild's Granddaughter

baptisms and marriages. Mom and dad were married at the Jackson Bay farm by Reverend Green, one of the respected and long-serving ministers of the coastal mission. Other couples we knew well, including Edie Hansen and Harold Bendickson, were married aboard one of the Mission boats. We particularly enjoyed Christmas visits of the Mission ship when the minister, Reverend Rollo Boas, sometimes with his wife and daughter aboard, led the singing of Christmas carols and distributed treats to the assembled children.

People who lived in the Port Neville area from the time it was first served by the Union ships, whose base was Vancouver, consulted a family doctor and a dentist in that city. Most people had a friend or relative living in Vancouver or New Westminster with whom they stayed during time spent away from home. Those who did not have someone "on the outside" had a favourite hotel or rooming house. Whichever the case, it became their home away from home.

The rest of the year women looked after the health of their families at home and some did so better than others. However competent her efforts, a woman could never replicate what was available in a hospital, or a doctor or dentist's office. For a hospital there was St. Michael's in Rock Bay, but it was at least eight hours away by boat even in fair weather. Unfortunately, that hospital closed in 1945 and became a home for the Graham family we knew well when we lived at Rock Bay. There was also a hospital at Port Hardy, but getting there from Port Neville involved a treacherous route across open water, which was not to be attempted in bad weather. Sometimes it seemed less dangerous to just stay at home and apply folk medicine, old fashioned remedies that had served well over many generations.

From a thick book found in most homes, often simply called the *Doctor's Book* people looked up the information they needed. Ours was a pale blue colour. For a burn from the stove a woman knew to spread butter or rendered fat, for a cut she learned where to apply pressure and perhaps a tourniquet if the slash was deep or long; for something in the eye a toothpick or thin smooth splinter of wood could be used to fold the eyelid back for easier removal of the offending speck. Eyewash solution was then applied, using a little plastic cup from the first aid kit found in every home, or at least at every camp office. Peroxide, iodine or other home solutions were commonly used to cleanse an open sore. *The Doctor's Book* held recipes for a poultice to draw a boil, and it showed diagrams and instructions on how to set and wrap a broken bone. Accidents did occasionally happen during the work day, and most families had at least one member who had studied first aid, even if not formally in a class.

At the beginning of cold weather every winter my mother dosed us daily with a spoonful of that hateful cod liver oil, the recommended nutritional supplement of the day. Anyone with a cold or stuffy nose received generous applications of Vicks VapoRub, and those with sore muscles, a similar application of smelly liniment.

Compared with other issues the people had to deal with, health care had a low priority. Providing the human necessities of adequate shelter, clean water, wholesome food and warm clothing needed to come first. From a genealogical perspective, people who had chosen to live on this remote coast needed to be strong stock. With exercise and fresh air a part of each day, most were generally healthy. All of what they needed could be supplied because there was work, and work yielded income to buy the essentials the family could not produce by itself.

Reflection:

When I think back to my childhood, and compare my expectations to what I observe in some young people today, I am concerned. The comparative ease of today's life has led to an expectation of the comfortable life, with little personal responsibility for actions, employment or care for others of the community. Where is the work ethic that kept immigrants pushing farther and farther west? There seemed to be a drive making people try harder each day to improve their lives and those of their families. Has it gone away? Where is the pioneering spirit that those of my age celebrate when we come together to study our personal history? And surely the most pressing question of all, where will the apparently overindulged, self-centred young people of today find needed strength when life's tempests come, as they surely will?

Port Neville PO building in 2002.

"I still enjoy writing and sending a hand written and addressed, stamped letter or card. With determination I make time to do it, because I know that in our busy email and text-message overwhelmed lives, the infrequent arrival of a "real letter" will add a bright spot to the recipient's day."

3.
Learning to Write

For children in the widely scattered population of remote coastal logging areas the most common form of early education was the British Columbia Elementary Correspondence School. In some larger communities or logging camps a cluster of families might find there were enough children among them to warrant a teacher. Then the main families would establish a school in an empty building, usually provided by the local logging company. If a family with several children moved away it could mean there were not enough students for the school to continue the next year so the remaining families simply returned to using the familiar correspondence lessons from Victoria.

My father's experience with school was less than stellar— he had not been a willing student. I have kept some report cards issued to him during years he attended a one-room school on Hardwick Island.

The Bendickson family, who settled on Hardwick, had arranged a school teacher for their children—Arthur, Barney, George, Jim, Harold and Linda—and had supplied the building for the school. Other children whose parents worked for Bendickson Logging or lived nearby were welcome to attend. It was at that little school that dad first met members of the Bendickson family, some of whom became mom and dad's lifelong friends. Several years ago my sister went to Hardwick Island with her husband and found the school building still standing in the same location, but long-since abandoned and surrounded by overgrown trees as nature reclaimed its own. The truth is dad had suffered through two years in the same grade so, at age thirteen and big for his years, the eldest Forberg son gave it up to go logging with his father.

His brother, Ingolf, continued farther in school than dad and I noticed later that books and magazines were always a big part of my uncle's solitary leisure time. Nano and Grandpa's eldest child, Elsie, was the only member of my extended family to graduate from high school, and after finishing went on to have a long career as a telephone operator in New Westminster, eventually retiring as supervisor.

My own first school experience was at our kitchen table, and much like other children doing correspondence lessons, my mother was the designated teacher of my officially taught school lessons. The only other child within a twenty-minute boat ride was my baby sister, Judy Lee, born January, 1943.

Mom's early schooling had begun while her family lived on an Alberta farm. She reminisced with us about riding a horse at a very early age in order to get to the local one-room school. In 1924, when she was 8 years old, mom moved to Vancouver with her parents and three brothers. Living in a city and attending a large school must have been a huge change for her.

At the school in Vancouver, mom completed Grade 8. During that time she became familiar with the Golinski family whose daughters, Vicki and Mary, became mom's close friends and, later, our lifelong family friends.

Adults in my close family were always generous with their time, reading me stories from the supply of assorted picture books sent as gifts by various friends and other family members. For an extended period of time, when I was only three, I was limited to bed by pneumonia. Part of the confinement was in a Vancouver Hospital; then, when I was well enough, my mother and I stayed with Granny Golinski. This meant that many of my early books became well-worn from heavy use during that time.

Mom was particularly adept at reading poems from *A Child's Garden of Verses*, by Robert Louis Stevenson. If she made a mistake I could correct her as I had memorized most of them. I still have that favourite book. Others included *Bambi* and *The Story of Little Goody Two Shoes*, which I also have and still treasure, inscribed as it is "from Muriel and Arthur, Kenny and Ruth," my parents' lifelong friends. My father could recite *The Billy Goats Gruff* by heart and without benefit of the pictures, since he remembered that favourite from his own childhood.

Despite what might seem to us an abbreviated education, mom and dad were both avid readers. I remember that they belonged to the Book of the Month Club, receiving at least one new hard cover volume in the mail each month for a few years. Searching the shelves one summer for something new to read, I found several of those very books, which undoubtedly stretched my reading capability. I especially recall *The Good Earth* by Pearl Buck and a then-popular and much discussed story, *The Egg and I*.

So it was that in September of 1944, just six weeks after my sixth birthday, I began Grade 1 with my mother as teacher. I have no idea what she thought about this new role but, given she had no choice I can only assume she accepted it just as she had the necessary move from her family's Jackson Bay farm to the much more constrained life on water when she married my father.

Although there had been few opportunities for socialization with other children my own age, there was no doubt I was ready for school. I had the benefit of a loving, attentive family who had prepared me with books and crafts for my first more formal learning. Pre-school systems were not common then, even in the towns and cities.

As I have explained, mail and supplies were delivered to the Port Neville government dock by the Union Steamship SS *Cardena* every two weeks. Late in August of that first year of education a huge brown paper-wrapped parcel of school supplies arrived from the Elementary Correspondence School in Victoria. It was a significant event; I took great pleasure in examining everything it contained. It was exciting to smell the new paper, pencils, erasers and books that spilled out of the package. As I did at the beginning of every school year thereafter, I enjoyed handling each of the new and always-changing school-related items.

Mom had just removed four loaves of fresh-baked bread from the oven and their aroma filled the kitchen. I examined new crayon colours, wondered at the small metal box of paints with its own paintbrush, and through their pictures, reviewed the possibilities of the new-to-me books, all in anticipation of being allowed to use these wonderful, precious new tools. My first examination of school supplies complete, Mom said, "Put those things aside now, Myrtle, it's time for lunch and you can begin work tomorrow morning," and handed me a thick end slice of the fresh bread. From that day onward, I looked forward with anticipation to each new chapter of my learning.

On "school days" I sat up to the red laminated kitchen table, on a structure the correct thickness to lift me into the right position for writing and reading. We had tried various pillows and boxes and finally settled on the perfect arrangement: a wooden box that had come into the house the Christmas before, filled with what we knew then as "Jap" oranges, was placed on one of the kitchen chairs. It was my designated seat until I grew some, and then the orange box was replaced by the big blue *Doctor's Book*. The surface of my desk was a forerunner of Arbourite, and its edge was finished with a thick band of shiny chrome. As soon as breakfast was over, and the dishes were done, I took my place at that table.

My teacher was punctual about following the school year according to the schedule sent from Victoria, just like other children did in a "real school." We began work each morning at nine, and except for our lunchtime break, we seldom finished before three. Somehow, mom also ??? managed to complete most of her indoor chores, including watching over my sister Judy's activities, and the cooking, baking, washing and cleaning. She was an acknowledged master of dovetailing, that practice used by all capable women.

First she read to me the instructions in the lesson package and then left me to do what it said while she carried on with her main job for the day. Each lesson package we received included a practice period for every new part of my learning, and that even meant printing (writing) answers to their questions and then completing the same section again for a "good copy" that we sent to supervising instructors in Victoria.

What did happen, however, was that I sometimes worked through the lessons more quickly than the time suggested for each part of the lesson package. It meant that over the months I got ahead for my age. By the end of the second school year I had finished Grade 2, and was already working on Grade 3 lessons. In this way I edged through four grades of school in three years, meaning that when I entered Grade 5 at Rock Bay School I was a year younger than the other pupils beginning Grade 5.

The age difference followed me all through school, to the point when I entered university at age sixteen.

With my home teacher firm about maintaining regular school hours, it left weekends free for us to do other things. I'm sure Mom was happy for a break from being indoors with me, for she was a committed outdoorswoman who would have preferred any outdoor, more physical, activity once her home-making chores were finished. I, on the other hand, would have happily sat at my schoolwork every day.

As she was strict in maintaining the school day she was also determined to have me present myself at the table/desk properly dressed and groomed. My widow's peak hairline has always been a particular annoyance in its desire to fall forward and over the years many techniques have been tried to tame it.

"Come on Myrtle; let me comb your hair before school." It was half past eight on Monday morning, and my mother stood before me, armed with brush, comb, two elastics and a bottle of Dippity Do.

"Hop up there and I'll get those stray bits out of your eyes," she said. Mom was not a tall woman, barely five feet, and she found it easier to stand behind me when she did my hair, while I sat on a chair where I would wiggle less. Lately, she had taken to styling it in French braids and was currently perfecting her technique. First came the part, a straight line from my forehead down the centre of my head. It sometimes took a few tries for her to get it right, at least to her standard.

Next, she gathered up a small triangle of one side of the shorter hair in front and combed some of the green goop through it. By having me tip my head back against her bosom, she could divide that hair in three and begin braiding. We both knew that this first part was the most difficult, for both of us, but when done well (and that meant pulled tightly), the braids would stay in place and look fresh for several days.

"Ow, that hurts!" I would wail.

"Hold still now, while I get these bits behind your ears I know it pulls, but I won't need to do this again tomorrow. That will mean you can be ready earlier to go with your dad to meet the boat." Tuesday was Boat Day.

Soon she was working on the other side of my head, and the whole agony began again. I breathed a sigh of relief when she was finally pulling up sections of longer hair at the back of my head, and working down to the neck. It was nearly over. Sometimes she pulled a few stray hairs while attaching the elastic at the end of each braid. My own daughters probably don't realize that the soft, covered elastics they sometimes use to make their own "ponytails," became available only long after my braids were being made.

"There, it wasn't that bad this morning was it?" She was re-assuring herself, I thought, but at least it was over for today and I was ready for school.

When each unit of work was complete, I felt great satisfaction watching my mother address the returning envelope: Elementary Correspondence School, Parliament Buildings, Victoria, B.C. Mom eventually taught me to write the address, but first she taught me to print. She showed me how to hold the fat, red pencil she had whittled to a point, using her whetstone-honed paring knife. The thick, soft lead required frequent sharpening as I practiced the steps, according to her instruction. The blank paper I used was a pale oatmeal colour with a characteristic pulpy texture. My practice, combined with her persistence, proved fruitful: I slowly learned to correctly shape the letters of the alphabet. Then, when I could form the letters more or less consistently, she promoted me to working on paper with lines.

Although stiff and rough, this new paper had alternate solid and dotted lines. It allowed a pupil to more accurately establish the correct height for each letter. Capital letters were printed two spaces high, but the smaller letters, the ones without a "leg" going either up or down, required only one space. Teachers began using terms such as "upper case" and "lower case" long after I had learned to write.

For practice, mom assigned printing a whole row of one capital letter, and then a whole row of that same letter in the non-capitalized form. If some of my shapes were a bit ragged, I could try another row, following a tried and true adage, "practice makes perfect." I'm not as sure about that as I may have been then. Allowing one day for learning each letter of the alphabet, meant my perfecting the printing of all twenty-six characters took weeks of dedicated effort.

When I had mastered the shaping and heights of each letter, my next writing lesson consisted of printing within the lines on standard lined paper, without the dots. We called this smoother paper "foolscap," and the resulting letters were considerably smaller.

I had barely perfected the forming of printed words when my mother insisted that I begin using those printed words to write letters. During my school day the practice of writing sometimes had a greater purpose than simply perfecting the forming of the letters and words. Although our contact with other people was rare, and always cause for celebration of some sort, mom was also teaching me the importance of etiquette, and that included creating my own "thank you" notes. After each Christmas and birthday, the requisite personal letters of thanks were sent.

Myrtle, Gunhild and Judy.

So began a lifelong practice of writing letters. I still enjoy writing and sending a hand written and addressed, stamped letter or card. With determination I make time to do it, because I know that in our busy email and text-message overwhelmed lives, the infrequent arrival of a "real letter" will add a bright spot to the recipient's day.

By Grade 3, I was considered ready to write script, and the esteemed Mr. MacLean entered my life. His penmanship methods were taught to all pupils in British Columbia from the 1920s to 1960s. Marching across the top of every blackboard in BC schools was Mr. MacLean's version of both the large and small letters. I first observed this when I began school at Rock Bay.

The MacLean Method of Writing was a carefully regulated formula for shaping letters, in order to meet an acceptable uniformity. Pupils were provided with workbooks in which they were expected to practice. The standard shapes were to be copied row by row on the pages. I suppose the goal was for all schoolchildren to emerge from Grade 8 with uniformly legible handwriting. It would have been a miracle had it happened so easily. I am apparently one of the system's failures.

The Elementary Correspondence School had established a strict MacLean system for answers to the lessons. As pupils, and for every subject, we were required to write out our answers in full sentence form, once for practice, and then rewritten in our best handwriting. The latter was submitted by mail for correction—and handwriting counted. As an early-developing writer, my handwriting met the expected standard; it no longer does. In contrast, until she suffered an immobilizing stroke, my mother's handwriting and that of her contemporaries, was remarkably clear with the letters uniformly graceful and well formed.

My mother also taught me most of what I know of grammar and spelling. My spelling is still not consistently accurate. Even during high school, when a teacher attempted instruction on the parts of speech, and offered examples of the rules for their use, my thoughts returned to the little rhymes and songs mom had learned when she was a child at school. There was a light-hearted common sense about them, as long as you could remember the rhyming words, and it seemed so much less complicated than the explanations in the grammar textbook.

Among the songs she taught me was one about "*a, e, i, o, u.*" There were spelling rhymes too. "*I* before *e*, except after *c*," has served me well when writing cheques to The Receiver General of Canada. I've since learned that spell-check is dependable only if I am able to program the computer to acknowledge the appropriate version of the English language. Additionally the program does not correct for word usage. So, like many writers, I'm still learning to spell.

My apprenticeship in writing has taken me from learning my letters in mom's cozy floathouse kitchen, to creating essays in high school, producing university term reports, formulating policy books, revising and writing of high school textbooks, compiling family history and now writing memoir. Seventy years later I'm still learning to write. This creative practice called writing is truly the ultimate challenge.

Reflection:

On looking back I can easily acknowledge that I have always been drawn to learning, and my love for it continues to the present day, as I struggle to understand new computer programs and to use them with proficiency. Even now, September means the beginning of a new school year, as it did when I was a child, university student, high school teacher and mother of school-aged children. I'm attracted to displays of new school supplies and all the paraphernalia that present-day pupils think they need to begin each year. After the freedom of unscheduled summer days with their leisurely pursuits, in September my monthly schedule of meetings and group activities begins once more.

Not long ago I received my first postcard from my three grandchildren. It was addressed by their mother, stamped and mailed from their home to mine. Each of the two older children, four and three years old at the time, had printed a very good semblance of their name. It warmed my heart. When I was at a Canadian Federation of University Women (CFUW) annual meeting in Newfoundland during that summer I addressed and mailed a postcard to each of the grandchildren in return.

That was but the beginning. As each of the children progress in their learning to write and to read, they have begun sending me letters and messages from their Ipads, some even with photographs attached. So far I have been able to keep up to them, learning more new technologies, but it appears they will force me to continue learning to write.

4.
A Floathouse Christmas

During those early years of living on the BC coast, our lifestyle dictated that planning for Christmas required a long lead time. My family ordered gifts and supplies from Woodward's or Eaton's catalogue at least a month in advance and longer than that if we were making any of our gifts by hand. It was the same all up and down the coast where dependable arrivals of The Union Steamship vessels sustained the residents of the area.

Boat Day was a highlight of our life, when one of the men took our boat down the inlet to deliver outgoing mail at the Port Neville Post Office and then waited to bring back incoming mail and parcels after they had been sorted. Dad or Uncle Ingolf enjoyed a half-day away from camp and the opportunity to visit with other people also waiting for their mail and grocery orders.

When November winter days closed in on us, my mother began the seasonal baking. With supplies delivered and now at hand, mom began her preparations. For weeks our little kitchen was filled with an irresistible aroma of butter, sugar and spices while I was focusing on school work. She baked the fruitcakes, both dark and light, early and then wrapped them in heavy waxed paper and placed them to age in a tight-lidded square can. I have two of those English biscuit (cookie) cans still and the lids are still dependably tight for storing baking.

Mom made Christmas puddings early too, according to her mother's perfected recipe. I never understood why steamed plum pudding was so important, although its distracting aroma promised a delicious flavour. Our family didn't even eat it on Christmas Day. We were always too full of turkey and trimmings to enjoy a heavy, hot dessert. Instead, we had Jell-O, which mom sometimes whipped with evaporated milk or, for a special treat, stirred in miniature marshmallows or canned fruit. Our favourite was fruit cocktail, that sickly sweet canned mixture which invariably settled to the bottom. In my home economics class many years later I learned how to prevent the fruit from settling.

The steaming rich pudding mom had laboured over was heated and served on Boxing Day, after we had enjoyed cold turkey leftovers. At that meal we could savour it, with a dollop of rum sauce on top. The sauce was more like a thick white butter icing, well-laced with Demerara rum which my father insisted was the only acceptable way for it to be served. I think my mother gave away more of the puddings than we ever ate, and fruitcakes were presented as gifts too, but she made them just the same. Early on in my own married life I made similar cakes and puddings and gave some away as gifts to friends who did not bake. When some years later I discovered none of my children liked the dried fruit treats I had grown up with, I chose instead to use the time to making cookies we all liked.

As the days clicked along and Christmas neared, I knew time was growing short when mom began making cookies. Mom had learned that in any self-respecting family with Norwegian roots, tradition decreed that there be at least seven different kinds of cookies on hand. Being ready to receive company that might drop in was also an important part of the holiday festivities and Hazel Forberg took care to meet the expectation of her husband's heritage. Her Belgium-born mother, who had spent her early years as a child and wife in rural Alberta, had taught her that every housewife needed to always be ready to offer hospitality. Part of that was to have food ready to serve visitors.

The humorous part of following these traditions was that, in such a remote location of the coast, anyone who came to visit us came a long way by boat. Our only neighbours were dad's parents and brother. Except for a few of the hard-working people living in Port Neville Inlet, who might have stopped by on a Sunday, any of our other visitors sent a letter or message with friends to arrange their time with us and then it was during summer months when weather was more predictable.

Mom made a different cookie variety each day while I worked on my correspondence lessons at the kitchen table. It was difficult to concentrate with those aromas. I especially enjoyed her bird's nest cookies and occasionally she allowed me to help make them. The dough is similar to shortbread, which we formed into round balls, then rolled in chopped walnuts, and pressed down with a thumb before baking. After they cooled mom filled the indentation with her own blackberry jelly or raspberry jam.

My grandmother's house was also filled with the smells of Christmas baking. Nano's cookies were different from the ones mom made. My favourites were called *creullers*. First Nano mixed thin delicate dough which she rolled and cut into strips, then twisted and cooked in hot fat. Once the twisted shapes cooled, she powdered them with icing sugar and stored them very carefully in a container that would not crush.

My mother and Nano exchanged baking of course, and recipes, and we enjoyed varieties from both kitchens. Long after Christmas had come and gone mom would bring forth something from her stash. Despite limited space and no electricity she nevertheless found secret places to hide things.

My parents and a few of their closest friends exchanged what mom called "household gifts" at Christmas. Sending a gift that the whole family could enjoy validated their friendship and did not involve much money. It eliminated the need to agonize over appropriate choices for specific members of each family, and we knew every family was pleased to have another gift to unwrap. These offerings were usually something home made, and often included cookies and cake or pickles or jam. All gifts had to be wrapped and sent in the mail, so mom was busy with these Christmas preparations very early each year.

Mom was artistic, and very creative with available materials. I remember her making vases from Mason jars, coated with plaster of Paris, and decorated with seashells pressed into the plaster while it was still wet. A coat of clear varnish made the vase easy to keep clean.

One year, we inherited a wind-up gramophone with black vinyl 78rpm records. After months of use, the records became scratched and mom found a new life for them. Setting a Pyrex mixing bowl upside down on a baking tray, she placed the centre of the scratched black record over the bowl and put the whole thing into a low-temperature oven. In a short time the record melted and folded in flutes around the bowl. Removing the Pyrex bowl once the record cooled, mom would paint designs on the resulting black bowl and it became a fruit and nut bowl or flower planter.

Gunhild's Granddaughter

Another year she made mobiles from driftwood. Judy and I chose interesting-shaped, small pieces of wood among the beach debris, and mom buffed them with brown shoe polish. Next, she attached each piece to fine fishing line and carefully arranged them so that they would balance and not tangle when they were hung. Each of these creations required hours of beachcombing by my sister and me and long evenings of mom's careful adjustment of the various weights by lamplight.

Mom was able to do all manner of creative crafts and seemed to have a bottomless source for her talents. She sewed, knitted, and crocheted, embroidered and tatted. From a deep understanding of plants and flowers, her crepe paper roses were the most authentic I have ever seen. I'm sure in such remote and lonely location she was driven to find outlets for her need to create, and did it all with minimal financial resources.

In her later years, mom discovered oil painting. By then she had some personal income from the Canadian government and chose to spend it on paints and brushes to recreate the landscapes she loved and knew so well. To her family and friends, a gift of mom's work to display on their walls was the ultimate gift for any occasion.

As winter progressed, with its stormy seas and high winds, our family became more confined to the house. Rain didn't stop dad from going to work, but a high wind did, because blowing branches and pieces broken off from snags were a great danger to anyone in the woods. If blustery winds sent smoke back down the chimney, it was reassuring to know that dad had cleaned the chimneys in both cook stove and airtight heater. On those days my mother could be short tempered. If she was cooking or baking something we knew there had better be a good supply of dry wood available.

In bad weather, Pick-Up-Sticks, Tinker Toys, jacks, marbles, card games, puzzles and lots of books kept us occupied after I had finished my lessons for the day. At very low tides our entire float sat on the sloping beach, so we waited for a higher tide to do activities that needed a level floor.

As the December days ticked along, secrets buzzed in our house. Strangely-shaped parcels disguised in brown paper began to appear on Boat Day and would disappear quickly. The closet in my parents' bedroom was out of bounds year round, but as we grew older we discovered the secret hiding place. The closet had shelves on one side where mom stored the bed linen and extra blankets, but there was space in the far corner, beyond what we could see from the open door.

During the year, boxes on the shelf above the hanging clothes changed as birthdays came and went, but as Christmas neared the whole configuration of the closet seemed different. We were not tall enough to look without benefit of a chair, and mom was very careful to close the closet doors. Dad didn't, but she came behind and shut them after him. The door squeaked, so if we had tried to drag a chair up to peer into its depths we would have been caught red handed.

During the week before Christmas day there were many things to be done. Choosing a Christmas tree from a mossy bluff or a slash that was accessible from the beach was always a family affair. We took that important outing just a few days before Christmas so our carefully-selected, stunted pine tree would stay green at least until New Year's Day, when we took it down.

To keep the tree from drying out in our house, dad had his personal method of preserving the tree. One of several red fire buckets kept on the float became a tree stand when filled with rocks and then with damp sand, packed around the tree trunk. It seemed that each year we heard of another house fire attributed to a spark landing in a dried-out Christmas tree. In a house constructed entirely of wood, we were vulnerable.

Now dad spent most of his time around home with us and helped where he could. He didn't work in the bush, but sometimes rowed out to the kelp bed to jig a lingcod for supper, or on a low evening tide dug a bucket of clams in a familiar place along the beach. Clam chowder for supper was an easy meal to prepare in minimum time when mom was otherwise busy. Dad made sure there was a large stack of firewood cut and a supply of kindling ready so that there could be continuous heat in the oven to cook the turkey plus wood for our living room heater.

A few days before Christmas mom made several different kinds of pies: berry, apple, pumpkin, lemon meringue. Then, on Christmas morning, we were allowed to choose whatever kind(s) we wanted for our breakfast.

Mom cooked the cranberries into sauce several days ahead using double the sugar and less water than the recipe listed, I learned later when I tried to get it right. She cut the bread cubes for turkey dressing and tossed them with seasonings so that only chopped vegetables, an egg and moisture – water or oil – needed to be added on Christmas morning.

With the bustle of creating and wrapping gifts and the special baking she undertook, mom must have been terribly weary before it was even time to prepare the festive meals we so enjoyed.

On Christmas Eve we all assembled in our tiny front room to admire the tree, shake the packages to guess what was in them and listen to carols on the battery-powered radio. We all loved music but not one of us had a particularly talented or trained voice, so singing by us was not part of the celebration. Our tradition included a reading of *The Night before Christmas*, hanging our stockings and setting out a plate of cookies for Santa. Just before bedtime, each of us was allowed to choose one package from those arranged on the floor around the tree or hidden in the branches. Of course, the Santa gifts would be added before we woke in the morning, but having one gift to open the previous evening made the excitement easier to control and ensured we awoke later in the morning.

Upon waking we were allowed to tiptoe out of bed, get our filled stockings, and take it back into bed with us until mom and dad were awake. Dad was always the first one up on Christmas Day, as with most other winter mornings. At Christmas, and on really cold mornings, he lit a fire in the airtight heater in the front room. Unlike the kitchen stove, the heater was started cold because it needed constant refilling to keep it going.

Fortunately for us, the room heated quickly so once the heater was warm enough we were able to stand close to it to enjoy its warmth as we dressed. Pulling off our flannelette pyjamas, we delighted in dressing on the new matching Christmas outfit mom has sewed for my sister and me. Then the long-awaited day began.

Our parents had a firm rule, strictly enforced. Although we could take our stocking back to bed with us until the fires were going, we were never allowed to open anything from under the tree until after we had all eaten breakfast – the pies – the dishes were washed and put away and everyone was dressed. It was agony to wait for all this to be done. Mom used the extra time to dress the turkey and put it into the oven. When everyone was assembled in the front room dad passed out the gifts. That ritual took considerable time, even when there weren't too many parcels, because we watched what everyone else was opening, taking turns doing it.

My sister and I looked forward excitedly to the next part of Christmas Day, when we visited our grandparents' house on the adjacent float for the noon meal. On this day we were treated to an array of Norwegian specialties that my grandmother had prepared or bought. There was always *gjethost*, a brown coloured goat cheese I learned to like; pickled herring, sometimes served as *rollmops;* pickled pig's feet, dad's favourite; hardtack, Grandpa's specialty, with holes to be filled with butter; dark rye bread and always the special baking Nano had done. The best part about this meal was that we were allowed to eat what we liked best, with no restrictions. I now know it was a smorgasbord.

After returning home we had time to enjoy our new gifts without restrictions, or chores. With anticipation, I could begin one of my new books. Mom would be busy in the kitchen with dad maintaining the oven temperature and stoking the fires according to her needs. By the time the evening meal was nearly ready, Nano, Grandpa and Ingolf were at the door, ready to examine our new treasures.

Christmas dinner meant roast turkey, dressing, mashed potatoes, sliced baked yams with brown sugar and butter, Brussels sprouts, gravy, cranberry sauce, homemade pickles, and, for dessert, fruit Jello and shortbread. After leaving the table feeling very full, of course, it wasn't long before everyone admitted they were ready for their beds. As a special treat, I was sometimes allowed an extra hour of reading time in bed before mom extinguished the coal oil light.

Ingolf, Einar (Andy) Elsie, Gunhild (Nano), Einar Rise(Buster). .

Dad (Buster), Myrtle, Judy, Mom (Hazel).

Reflection:

As I look back I believe that it was actually my father who kept the spirit of Christmas best in our home. He made the week of Christmas a pleasant experience for all who lived there and for everyone who entered it. Grumpiness or complaints were not allowed and compliance to his well-established rule was achieved without a struggle. His calm approach to any potential discord, and his spirit of good cheer, overrode any other possibility. Love surrounded us all, between him and my mother, toward us by both of them, and in their welcome to our home to any visitors, both invited and otherwise.

I suspect my father learned it by example from his Norwegian immigrant parents I have discussed similar stories of calm and mellow goodwill of others from that culture.. His spirit of Christmas has left a lasting impression on me. In my own family, my husband and I have attempted to combine traditions from both of our families; I can only hope that we have been able to impart to our own children the same spirit of goodwill and understanding.

Hazel Forberg, Gunhild (Gunnulfson) Forberg.

5.
Grandparents and Extended Family

GUNHILD GUNNULFSON

Grandma Gunhild was an influential person in my early years. I called her White Nano, for the whiteness of her hair. My maternal grandmother was Little Nano. White Nano welcomed me to her cozy floating home beside ours and spent innumerable hours teaching me first steps of most of the needle-crafts that I have enjoyed through my life. In recent years, I have been drawn to the colours she favoured in the fabrics of her dresses. Rich shades of orange and yellow muted by greens and some browns, those colours serve to brighten the dreary grey sky of she found in her new Canadian home. Chosen from the catalogue and purchased by the yard, she sewed almost every-thing she wore, including the ever-present aprons that encom-passed her well-defined frame. With an all-business demean-our she held her shoulders square and her body upright, giving an impression of height. Whenever I slouched she showed me the way it could be corrected, by placing a broom handle across my back and hooked there by the bend of my elbows.

I remember her shoes. They were always black with sen-sible Cuban heels, and were carefully polished, worn with ugly thick beige stockings. I think they were knit of a cotton fibre mom called lyle. The only time I ever saw Nano wearing pants was when she joined us to walk the beach at low tide to dig clams. I still have a photo of her with heavy wool fishermen pants tucked into grandpa's heavy black rubber boots, and carrying a fire bucket. This is definitely not the ever-proper lady I adored.

A highlight of a visit to Nano's house was sharing coffee-time with her. There was such a ceremony to the process. First she stoked the fire in her wood-burning kitchen stove. Cold water from the creek came to the kitchen tap from which she filled the camp-sized, peculator coffee pot. At the same time, she refilled a large teakettle that resided at the back of the stove. All of the metal surfaces in her tiny kitchen were polished to a shine, including that huge kettle and all of the trim of the stove and its warming oven, above the stove's hot surface.

She poured coffee beans from a tight-lidded can into a well-worn wooden coffee grinder, the kitchen implement I had tried to locate after my parents died, thinking it might be among their or my sister's possessions. Success! Two years ago I discovered it among my eldest male cousin, Don's, treasures. With a few cranks of its handle, Nano's whole kitchen was filled with that wonderful aroma that I've coveted since then. Coffee is my primary addiction. She seemed to know just the right number of beans to grind so their grounds could be placed directly into the basket of the coffee pot without measuring or spilling. Then she settled the lid into place and positioned the pot on the hottest part of the stove, which I recognized as the smallest removable circle of the three used to access the firebox when wood was added. The coffee-making process begun, we could go on with the current lesson until the coffee pot came to the boil. Some days it was knitting, embroidery, or crocheting, but today's lesson was sewing.

At the Port Neville 'narrows,' on a low tide, abalone were plentiful then.

As my lesson proceeded, we eventually heard plop … plop … plop … and then the more rapid plop … plop … followed by plop, plop, plop, plop which meant it was time for Nano to pull the pot to the back of the stove before it boiled over. Our lesson interrupted, now the coffee clatch began as she set out the cups and saucers, spoons, sugar bowl and can of Pacific evaporated milk. Into my cup she poured milk from the can to at least half, then, when the blurping sounds of the pot had stopped, she added coffee from the steaming pot. I was allowed to add my own sugar, stir and test the temperature from a spoon.

Nano sipped politely from the cup edge and offered me a plate of her family-famous Norwegian cookies. As I grew older, the percentage of coffee to milk became greater until during my first year at university I eliminated milk altogether. I had forsaken sugar as a calorie saving measure long before then. On the other hand, my grandfather used generous amounts of both milk and sugar and occasionally slurped when he drank. I have since witnessed the same in other European-born people. I've seen some of them, whose cup is large with a wide matching saucer, pour a portion of the hot coffee into the saucer and allow it to cool before pouring it back into the cup to drink.

The matching cups and saucers Nano and Grandpa used on special occasions have recently come to my home from that of my sister. They are in a lovely burgundy and blue floral design and, in typical Scandinavian fashion, the Her size is much smaller than the His.

With Forberg grandparents, about 1946.

The coffee ceremony over, Nano and I returned to my current lesson – using a hand cranked sewing machine. I had watched Mom sew with hers, but the busy person she was left little time to teach me. Nano let me turn the handle while she fed the fabric under the pressure foot toward the needle. In time I graduated to handling the two edges of fabric pieces to make a strait seam using both hands, for example mending a torn sheet, while she watched me and slowly turned the handle for me. I have that sewing machine to this day and found it stronger and more dependable than my electric machine when I was working on heavy upholstery or plastic-coated fabrics for our new home.

Other times she showed me how to make different embroidery stitches that I could prac-tice on table and pillow covers. There was an inherent magic in watch-ing as she imprinted the bleached, flour-sack fab-ric with a chosen stitchery pattern by pressing its paper design upside down in place using a heavy *sad iron* that, in electricity-free remote

Nano mending Grandpa's socks.

areas were heated on a cook stove or heater for ironing. While the imprinted fabric cooled, we carefully made choices of embroidery thread colours that would best make the pattern. Then she showed me the appropriate stitches: outline for the stems, French knots for the flower centres and an intricate looping technique called detached chain, or lazy daisy stitch, for the leaves. I have a good supply of embroidery thread inher-ited from Nano's eldest child, Aunt Elsie, who, I can imagine, learned techniques from her mother like I did.

Grandparents and Extended Family

Sometimes my grandparents, with Uncle Ingolf, came to our home for an ordinary Sunday dinner or a birthday celebration. All the adults played cards and occasionally could be talked into a game of Snap, or Pairs, or Fish with us. After supper we played popular board games like Chinese checkers, Snakes and Ladders, or Monopoly, which everyone could enjoy.

The bunkhouse space of Dad's younger brother was my favourite retreat when I was tired of books or Judy's banging of pot lids. Uncle Ingolf always spoke to me as he would to an adult, and I could depend on him to have conversation with me about things I considered important. His shake-clad residence consisted of one large bare room containing four metal single beds, the extras for times when Forberg Logging hired help to get the work done or the family had overnight visitors. The wood-burning heater gave the room a smoky smell.

Ingolf was a smoker himself, as were most people around me, so the accoutrements from his habit, tobacco can, rolling papers, matches and ashtray, held a significant space on the desk-height table set under the window. I think he had made the table himself at school, possibly during one of the winters when Nano took her children to New Westminster to attend school there.

EINAR EINARSON FORBERG

I remember Grandpa Andy as an elderly gentleman, and recall being absolutely mesmerized by the process he went through each evening to prepare and smoke his everyday pipe. He was not a heavy smoker as other men of my family were, but the steps were predictable, akin to ritual. On special occasions he would use a traditionally-carved, long Norwegian pipe, festooned with red tassels attached to a cord from which the pipe hung on the living room wall.

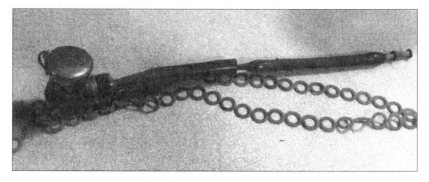

Grandpa's Norwegian pipe,
used in the evening on special days.

I would watch him lift it from the wall hook and pack the bowl with a pungent brand of tobacco, which he smoked only rarely. This one had quite a different aroma from the brand he regularly used. Seeing him hold the bowl almost at arm's length, sucking in to get the pipe started enough that we could smell the smoke, was a continually fascinating procedure for a little girl to observe.

Grandpa Andy was a big, strong man, from a life of hard labour, but he was not especially tall. By the time I was six, he would have been seventy-one, comfortable at home in his rocking chair, and though tired after his work in the bush, willing to make

Grandpa Andy and Dad
beside the 'donkey.'

room for me on his knee with a picture book. He appeared to enjoy watching his granddaughters, yet Grandpa Andy never said much, even in adult company. Whenever I hear the lilting accent of a Norwegian-born person, I remember again those infrequent conversations with him. Although he mastered speaking the English language, reading it was difficult for him and he made little effort to read much more than newspaper headlines. He did read a Norwegian magazine that arrived regularly in the mail.

THE FEARINGS

It wasn't until after my parents died that I set out to learn more of my family's history—I, like many people, made the same mistake of waiting too long. I began by joining a family history interest group of Canadian Federation of University Women (CFUW) members; when they planned a trip to Salt Lake City I accompanied them. In the huge Mormon Family History Library, I quickly discovered how much easier it was to research relatives when I could read files in English. I had tried the Norwegian Forbergs but gave it up on that trip.

Working from my Grandpa Bill back through the generations, I learned that his original immigrant ancestor, John Fearing, had come from England and landed near Boston approximately ten years after the Mayflower arrived. The extended lines of people along the Eastern seabord who were descendants of John Fearing had been thoroughly researched and written about in English, so it was an easy beginning to my family history research. When I had travelled with my mother, years before, to the little town of Hingham near Boston, Massachusetts, and met Mom's cousin Myrtle, my impression was that the family was large and well respected. On that trip I also learned that the children of William Francis Fearing were the last of Grandpa Bill's father's line.

My grandfather had travelled across the continent from Hingham, and when he neared the West coast had heard that free land was available in Alberta. He travelled North, established himself on a chosen plot of land and proved it up, a term used to mean to clear and till the raw land within the time allowed. In Alberta, he met my grandmother, Katie Clooten, who had come as a girl with her family from Belgium, and across the prairies in a covered wagon. Researching Nano's roots in Belgium was more difficult, because of the language issue, but with the help of several library researchers I was able to go back through several generations of Clootens.

I was reassured, by knowing about my Fearing grandparents and where they had come from, but it has taken me a long time to understand the reason for the ambivalence I have felt about many of the Fearing relatives I know. The truth is that those I have known were fundamentally different from the Forbergs, with whom I spent so much of my time. I would characterize the Forbergs as having been more proper, more formal in the typical European sense. The Fearings, on the other hand, seemed more focused on plants, animals, husbandry, crafts and tilling the land. I did not always appreciate some of their rough language and in the case of my mother's brothers, their sense of humour. Ab and Chuck were similar in their attempts to be funny; Uncle Bill, Mom's youngest brother, was more restrained and over the years I spent enjoyable time in Vancouver with him and his wife Gladys. They and their son Ron, with whom I had an on-going good friendship, welcomed me to their home overlooking the ocean-side train tracks near Hastings Park.

Despite the differences in grandparents and my occasional discomfort with the Fearings' rough manners I learned a great deal about life during the summers I spent at the Jackson Bay farm and again after the senior Fearings had moved to Campbell River. During Grade 11, I bunked with them for the summer when I held a job at Pat's Style Shop. That year Nano showed me how to hook rugs using cut strips of old woollen fabric. Her rugs were well known around the area, and I still have a beautiful floral one displayed on the floor in our guest room. She was also famous for managing to keep houseplants blooming, especially African violets and cacti. I have some of each with lesser results, but I always think of Nano Katie when I water and feed them.

A goodbye to the Jackson Bay farm families.

At the farm, Little Nano (so called because she was short while White Nano was taller and had white hair) led the weeding brigade each morning in her vegetable garden, and taught

Gunhild's Granddaughter

me the differences between tiny chickweed plants and her sprouting vegetables. Except for my cousin George, I was the eldest child at the farm but we were all expected to help each according to age and ability. Both Nano and Grandpa Bill tried to teach me to milk a cow, with only marginal success. It was with them that I discovered the miracle of fresh milk, and because it was so unfamiliar, raised on diluted canned milk as we were, I wasn't sure I liked it at all. I still don't like milk, but that has no bearing on whether it is canned or fresh.

What I really enjoyed after the milking was done was being allowed to run the hand separator. Best of all was thick cream on berry pies and other fruit desserts that were regular fare at the farm.

Another event that seemed magical was when Nano, or Ab's wife Beverly, made butter from some of the chilled thick cream. Having been raised on the farm, my mother always looked forward to a tall glass of cold buttermilk, which to this day I appreciate only for its ability to leaven and flavour baked goods.

My primary chore at Jackson Bay Farm was the chickens—feeding grain to them twice daily and once each day gathering their eggs. Grandpa Bill was in charge of selecting which of the hens was next in line for the stew pot or roasting pan because she had quit laying. When he had made the decision, all of the cousins assembled at the woodhouse to watch as he stretched her neck over the chopping block and with one swift axe movement removed the head. I learned how to pluck a chicken (Nano made the best feather pillows) and how to eviscerate one, all useful lessons for times when my husband came home with ducks or grouse he had shot to be served for dinner. These days this might seem unusual, but I have come to consider it just one more part of my education in food preparation.

On the boom at Jackson Bay with all my cousins.

When there was a break from chores of weeding, feeding, picking, shucking, plucking, canning, and keeping track of
the little ones, I was allowed to choose a book from those Aunt
Beverly had kept from her school days. She had a whole shelf
of good ones, some that I read and reread and became my best
friends. It was a welcome relief to find a quiet corner on the hon-
eysuckle-covered porch and, uninterrupted, just enjoy the story.

All of my cousins agreed that the very best part of being at
the Jackson Bay farm for part of the summer was the haying season. For days, Grandpa Bill tapped the barometer and checked
the skies morning and evening, announcing after each that it
wasn't time to cut yet, it might rain. Then, when he was assured
by his trusted barometer and some personal internal signal, that
the time had come, (there being no weather reports), he and
Uncle Ab took turns running the tractor to cut the hay.

The next stage involved more waiting, watching the skies,
hoping for sunshine and breezes. If luck was on our side the hay
would be drying, if not it might rain and then there would be even
more waiting. After several good dry days the real work began.

Depending on how many pitchforks were available, Grandpa and at least two of his sons, with me and cousin George as part-time workers, set to work overturning the hay. Hot and sticky and covered in seeds as we were, it seemed to take forever.

That finally done, there was another wait time of several days before Grandpa Bill pronounced the hay was finally dry. If taken in too soon and not thoroughly dried, it would rot in the barn, or heat up and possibly cause a fire.

The barn and hay loft were usually out of bounds for us to play in, but for several weeks prior to haying time we were allowed there—most of the stored hay had been used up. Now the bit left was a small pile remaining on the floor below the loft, so with ropes for climbing and swinging fastened in place, the most courageous of us took to jumping from the loft into the pile. After each safe drop we would climb up the rickety ladder to do it all over again. Even for the littlest cousins it was great fun.

When the tractor revved its engine again, we were once more called to help pitch the dried hay on to its trailer. Higher and higher the load became until the tired old trailer would hold no more; the tractor waited for us to pile on and find a space atop of the hay. It smelled wonderful but prickled and scratched. This was not a day to wear shorts. The ride across the field back to the barn was the most fun of all, with everyone screaming and laughing over the bumps. When we arrived at the barn, the men unloaded the hay into the loft while we rested until it was time to go out for the next load. Even a ride in the empty trailer was a treat. Again and again the process continued until a mealtime break was called. With luck, it would be a good crop of hay that year and would take more than a day to bring in. If so, we could get to have the same fun the next day. Regardless, during haying adults and children alike were always ready for their beds at the end of the day.

Reflection:

It has always distressed me to think that while I grew up with full benefit of a complete family of two sets of grandparents and assorted uncles and aunts, my father had none of those benefits of relatives near him, and my mother, to some extent, knew most of her extended family but not her grandparents. When I have these thoughts, I am ever grateful that I have ready access to my own grandchildren and am able to impart to them some of the important life lessons my own grandparents gave me.

6.
At Home in Rock Bay

In July of 1947, the Forberg camp floats had been towed south down Johnstone Strait from Port Neville, and secured to Thurlow Island where they were protected by Turn Island, just across from Rock Bay. I assume the move had been initiated when the timber sale Forberg's were working on at Port Neville was completely harvested. An additional reason would have been to make it easier for me to go to a real school because beginning in September, and for those first four school months of 1947, my father ferried me to the Rock Bay dock in the morning and back to our floathouse at the end of my school day. His commitment to my schooling took a significant chunk of time from his workday.

As a hand logger, he worked according to his own clock and it was a source of pride to him that he answered to no one. Within the partnership of Forberg Logging, his main responsibility was making up the booms, a job that had to be done when the tide was right. Because it dominated his work schedule, I learned how to read a tide table at a very young age, and even now I'm aware of tidal movements when I glance seaward from my present home.

Before my folks were married, mom's father and my dad constructed the house I lived in as a child; thanks to the supporting skids it was possible for it us to live in the same house as before, pulled up on land. Rock Bay was my home from nine until I left to attend high school in Campbell River at thirteen.

Our same house moved to land at Rock Bay.

My family made the physical move to Rock Bay during the winter of 1948. In the space of a January weekend our home was relocated. A tug towed our floathouse across Johnstone Strait on the seasonal high tide and pushed it up to the gravel shore beside the Rock Bay government dock. The skids that supported the cross beams underneath the floor proved useful when a large Caterpillar tractor, owned by Granite Bay Timber Company pulled our two-bedroom home off the float and across the beach onto land. Then, with much gesturing and shouting of instructions by my father and company employees, our house was turned and positioned the way mom and dad wanted it.

Next to be pulled across the beach into position beside our house came the colour-matched woodshed, with its jaunty lean-to roof. In this location we no longer required the outhouse, so it was left to stand lonely out there on the old float until the raft holding our other leftovers, the wire fence, board decking and smaller flowerboxes, lifted off the beach at high tide to be towed away for other users. Mom had asked the men move her biggest two boxes off the old float and settled them at the edge of the bank beside our house so that she could attempt to create a flower garden once more.

As soon as the house was in place and level, dad connected our water pipe to the community water system bringing water to us from higher up the creek, beyond tidal flow, and positioned a larger pipe that allowed kitchen and bathroom waste to spill into the mouth of the creek. Later that year he installed a real flush toilet and, to his large frame, a miniature, metal shower enclosure.

View from the kitchen window.

After ten years of being surrounded by water with only ducks and seagulls to watch on the water, Mom had an entirely different view from that same kitchen window as she worked at the sink. It must have been a strange new world for her, being at the centre of the action in a busy camp and seeing successive logging trucks dump their monstrous loads into the mouth of the creek. Ocean water filled up the creek during high tide, so the boom men could push the logs to the ocean for sorting. Once the logs were in the deeper water, other boom men separated the logs by species to make up full booms of each. On more than one occasion, when the boom crew needed help, my father helped.

When the logging camp was first established, the area between the creek bank and a small island we now called "The Rock," had been reclaimed by dumping rocks and fill to create a useful flat space beside it. In its new location, the little house I had always known as home was perched on a narrow strip of land that had originally been swamp at low tide and covered with shallow water at high tide.

Thanks to this land reclamation, The Rock was no longer an island, and it became my favourite retreat. The outer reaches of the craggy mound I thought of as my personal space was covered with wild roses, whose blooms and delicate fragrance in May kept me returning. Before long, the same plants yielded tasty nibbles in the form of gigantic rose hips. Mom encouraged me to pick these for her to make jelly, something I have recently made for a grandson who likes it best of all the jellies and jams I make. Best yet were the succulent wild strawberries that, in July, hid along the edge of the rock surfaces; no taste of any fruit was comparable. On the mossy surface of that timeless rock I could lie flat, out of the wind, and, for a change, be alone with my imagination.

Rock Bay in 2002.

Gunhild's Granddaughter

I frequently hiked up, following the narrow path that cir-
cled the rock and felt like I was truly on top of the world. If you
saw The Rock you would know otherwise. From its peak I had a
full 360 degree view. I remember one day when I looked across
Johnstone Strait to the small protective island behind which
our floathouse had been tied before we moved. Turning to the
right, southward down Johnstone Strait and then nearer, I saw
completed booms secured to piles that formed corners of the
booming ground. Farther to my right was a boom being built
by *pike-pole* wielding boom men and a line of trucks dropping
their loads at the busy log dump. Each time a loaded truck came
to a stop, the dump machine roared to life, and I could see its
operator hook to the load, put the machine in gear and by its
sound knew the load would soon rise up, swing over the dump
and be released into the creek below. Across the hill, above the
dump, were two rows of houses occupied by families we eventually knew well, all subjected to the high pitched noises of
what was happening at the dump below.

When I faced our home, there was the woodshed roof,
our little house with cream-coloured shake siding. Beyond it to
the other side of the narrow bay were two big bunk houses, nes-
tled under a moss-covered hill. Between the bunk houses and
our home lay a grassy parking lot where people leaving Rock
Bay by boat left their cars and trucks, then a wide roadway, a
plank wood walk, the cookhouse and access to the pier. Over
the top of our house I could see a gravelled logging road that cut
into the verdant forest and led on fifty miles south to Campbell
River. This was our way out to the world beyond. For the first
time, we had neighbours unrelated to us and freedom to travel
by road.

I had been aware for a long time that there were places that had modes of transportation which were not water dependent. At least once each year I had travelled by steamboat to Vancouver with my mother. In the city, I rode on streetcars and even in an automobile: my Aunt Elsie's friend, Cliff, had a shiny black Packard we rode in once.

Walking a Vancouver street with Mom.

Gunhild's Granddaughter

Our two-week stay in Vancouver always involved a visit to the doctor and dentist. An examination by an elderly medical doctor in his Burrard Street office was mandatory, but Mom eventually gave up trying to convince me to let the dentist work on my teeth. I was eighteen years old, attending university, before I could gather the courage to allow a dentist to fix a cavity. It was always the drill vibration that got to me, and it still does.

In Vancouver I enjoyed riding the streetcar to go shopping, but I didn't much enjoy being dragged through Woodward's Hastings Street department store while Mom looked at everything. She did her real purchasing back at home by carefully making selections from the Woodward's catalogue, which arrived in the mail.

On the streets and streetcars there were interesting people, and things to look at, but the best part of going shopping was sitting up to the Woolworth's lunch counter where Aunty Gladys worked. I was allowed to order and then devour a delicious banana split. Ice cream on the floathouse was never a possibility, unless we made it with canned milk on a snowy day. But the world of ice cream and streetcars was not my world. We lived differently than they did in the city and I had never imagined it would become my own reality. Once we moved to Rock Bay, it seemed it might be.

During the autumn of 1947, it had taken a while for me to get used to the new routine of Rock Bay. For those first four months, my home was in a different location than the rest of my fellow students, who lived on Vancouver Island, while I slept in our floating home across Johnstone Strait. Sometimes in the afternoon, if my father was delayed coming for me, I waited in the freight shed, out of the rain. I enjoyed poking around inside the big covered space and reading the labels on items left there, or, if the shed was empty, reading the names and messages people had written on the walls. The shed's shiny metal construction protected travellers and their luggage from inclement weather while waiting for the Union Steamship vessel *Cardena* to dock, or for their family member's or company's boat to come pick them up.

Without fail, every second week, the *Cardena* arrived and deposited people and supplies on the float. Everything delivered had been ordered by mail several weeks previously, as it had been when we were at Port Neville. I had only ever known this method of delivery of mail and supplies but, here at Rock Bay, I was learning that some people lived another way – there was a road here.

One day, Mr. Hazzard, our teacher, marched us all down to the end of the dock to witness this part of commerce and mail service. "The thing to remember," he explained, "is that all up and down the coast, where there are no roads, this is the only way people can get their supplies. For them, their mainstay of transportation and communication service is the Union Steamship boats. The smaller boats coming in today are picking up parcels that folks living out on the outer islands ordered two weeks ago. I know that some of you drive into Campbell River with your parents to shop for groceries and clothes, but I wanted you to see how most of our mail arrives here."

For my classmates, this little expedition became a combined geography and science lesson all in one. For me it had always been exciting to witness the union boat's arrival, and to watch people going about their business of unloading or loading, sending or receiving. This process was one of the few things about Rock Bay that was not new to me and being able to answer questions about it helped make me more acceptable to some of my classmates.

The familiar Union Steamship company ceased operating in 1959, while we lived in Rock Bay. It was a sad time for those of us who had grown up depending on its unwavering schedule. With the increasing popularity of radio phones, communication systems were changing and people could now call for a floatplane. Many families now had a high-powered speedboat that could take them where they needed to go, or at least someplace where there was a road connection to the outside world, like we had now. Soon after we settled in at Rock Bay our little house was connected to a phone line with a big black thing attached on the kitchen wall. Two longs and a short gave us the operator, who would connect us to anyone available on the Campbell River line.

After three years of correspondence lessons, being in a school building with other children held many new experiences. Now I was able to walk home for lunch, and then go back up the hill for the remainder of the school day.

Not only was I with some children my own age during school hours, but living in the same community with them and their families meant I could visit with them after school and on weekends. I was beginning to learn to play with them. Until we moved, I had rarely been around other children other than my Fearing cousins, and, except for George, and Ron in Vancouver, only those younger than I was.

Of course, I missed seeing Nano and Grandpa daily, and especially spending weekend time with Nano in her kitchen and at the hand-cranked sewing machine that she taught me to use. Grandpa finally retired from logging and they had purchased a home on Thulin Street in Campbell River about the time we moved our house to Rock Bay. During the summer holiday, we made the dusty car trip to see them at their new home. Following a life long tradition of being beside them, Uncle Ingolf was building his own house in the same block on Thulin Street where they now lived.

At Nano's new house, there was a big yard with a beautiful flower garden she was obviously enjoying. On their float she had worked hard to make a garden in wooden boxes. She and Mom had created soil from rotted seaweed they picked from the beach after storms and occasionally went ashore to scrape mulch from under the evergreens. Nano was proud of the healthy blooming dahlias and gladiolas surrounding the door of her floathouse home in summers. Having real soil available to her now was so much better she could even grow vegetables.

The Forberg grandparents' home on Thulin Street.

From our central location in the Rock Bay camp, my family could watch all the activity around us. My five-year-old sister, Judy, restrained by a gated, covered porch along one side of the house, became fascinated by the variety of traffic passing in front of her. From that vantage point she could see almost everything happening in the community and with her watching while I was at school, she learned details about everyone.

During the work week, logging trucks constantly unloaded at the dump, settled their trailer in the empty position and disappeared in a cloud of dust up the gravel road for another load. At quitting time, each driver parked his truck in the shop, located beyond the bridge that spanned the creek, where it would be greased and fuelled by a mechanic working the afternoon shift. Judy reported on cars arriving to deliver the people leaving by boat or picking up those arriving. At times, the grassy open space beside our house was a crowded parking lot with drivers leaving on the same boat as their passengers. Eventually we learned the owners' names and what kind of car they drove.

As do most people who spend much time on or near the ocean, we came to recognize anyone who came into the bay by the design or name of the boat they owned. Sometimes, when boats were tied at the Rock Bay dock, their owners left them and drove away for the weekend. We came to know at which camp they worked and whether the camp was on a ten-day-on-four-off shift, or the more common, weekday-on and weekend-off, as Granite Bay Timber in Rock Bay was.

There was a regular parade of men going to and leaving the cookhouse at mealtime, men stopping at the timekeeper's shack for their pay or first aid treatment of some kind, and owners and managers going to and from the company's guest house beside us. Occasionally, the camp manager even had a lady friend come to visit him – noted for fancy clothes, polished high-heeled shoes and the makeup she wore.

Mom's clothesline stretched to a tall pole at the edge of the creek, in front of the parked cars beside our house. If the wind blew the wrong way our clean clothes were directly in line for a coating of the dust created when the logging trucks headed back up the gravel road. Sometimes she chose to do her wash on the weekend when the trucks were parked, but of course she still had to deal with the dust of moving cars. I remember my mother grumbling about the clouds of dust those bulky multiple wheeled logging trucks stirred up in the dry weather.

"Just look at that mess, Myrtle. I had to do the wash today because it was piling up and now I may as well not have bothered," she said. She had been busy sewing matching dresses for Judy and me all that week so she really didn't need additional aggravation.

First taste of freedom a – Birthday bike!

"Maybe it will rain tomorrow and wash the dirt away," I offered. Much to her annoyance, the wind had just changed direction again.

I remember the bike my parents gave me for my tenth birthday that July. It was a turquoise green Raleigh with a low-slung front bar designed for girls, because in those days girls always wore skirts. It featured the latest of balloon-style tires advertised to be easier to manage and to give a smoother ride. There seemed to always be bumps and ruts in the rough gravel in front of our house, so the best riding was when the camp road had just been graded. That was often on Friday, which gave a smoother ride for those leaving for the weekend. The smoothest ride to be had was along the boards on the dock. Learning to ride that bike was a real challenge for me, as I had never been particularly athletic nor did I crave physical activity as my mother and sister did. After a few scrapes and bruises, I eventually got the hang of it. To this day I'm not enthusiastic about bike riding although many of my friends are, but at the time it gave me independence that even then I was beginning to treasure.

My sister turned out to be quite unlike me in both her interests and abilities. As soon as she was old enough to be released from her porch prison she rode her new tricycle like a pro, and during her life went on to excel in a great many sports and athletic activities. By the time she was involved in them my favourite pastime had become reading, and still is.

With our house in this new location, we surveyed an amazing array of moving things and people. After nine years of being only with parents, sister, uncle and grandparents, this sudden transition was mesmerizing. I had made my first step toward living on land, and with the ability to still see water on both sides of the house, I loved it.

Reflection:

Because of those early years, the ocean became a significant part of who I am. I absolutely love being on the water, whether it's in a small boat, a ship, a barge, a seaplane or even standing on a dock. Viewing an open expanse of ocean calms me and assures me that I'm capable of facing any challenge. In retrospect I've come to understand that those earliest experiences have influenced where I would chose to make my home, and even where I would spend leisure time.

Although I did not realize it at the time, now after a lifetime, I realize just how significant was my family's relocation to Rock Bay. That move turned out to be the first in a series of transitions from the water-dependent world into which I had been born, to a land-dominated world in which I would live the remainder of my life.

This summer I have recreated an area of my garden that, as with all older garden plots, had become tired and overgrown. From my patio and windows, it has become more important to have a pleasant frame for my ever-present sea view. On the raised seaside burm, I planted variegated greenery, winter blooming heathers and have all-season varieties of yellow-tipped cypress, giving me a bright and cheerful outlook even on the dreariest of grey, winter days. Having an ocean view to enjoy is still my first priority.

Gunhild's Granddaughter

7.

A Rock Bay Christmas

T he Rock Bay school building itself sat on skids, like our own house, just in case the number of children dropped below the few needed to keep the school open. If that happened, the owner could move it away to some other small community that needed a school.

This fall term I was one of the two pupils in Grade 6; Mickey Jay and I used the same reader and tackled the same arithmetic problems, then shared science and social studies lessons with Grade 7 students. Twenty-eight was the highest number of children enrolled during my four years at Rock Bay School. Some years there were only twenty. As well as children of the families living in this camp, who walked the short distance to the school, others from a nearby logging camp were bussed in every morning. Those students were cousins having the family name of Jay, sons and daughters of five brothers who had grown up in Victoria on the southern tip of Vancouver Island. Jay Brothers Logging at Little River, just north of Rock Bay, was a family-run operation much smaller than Granite Bay Timber, the logging company where we were.

The annual school picture.

Gunhild's Granddaughter

The teacher's position must have been lonely. With the exception of Mr. Hazzard, my first teacher in Rock Bay, who stayed for several years because he seemed to enjoy the rural lifestyle and outdoor activities, the teacher who sent us off for summer holidays in June was not the one who greeted us in September. Sometimes a replacement teacher came part way through the year. Room and board was provided by the Graham family who lived in the former Rock Bay Hospital.

The same teacher taught every subject for grades one to eight and we all shared responsibility for the smooth running of the school. As two of the older students Micky and I were expected to assume some responsibility for the younger children. The oldest boys kept the oil stove adjusted, and, when needed, cleaned the chimney. At least they weren't required to chop wood and kindling as were kids in many rural schools. Older girls wiped the blackboards and cleaned the brushes at the end of the day. Some of us helped the younger children with coats and boots.

On a wet day the classroom steamed with the scent of black rubber boots and yellow slickers. On winter days, we shivered in our seats. In this temporary location, the base of the building had not been enclosed, leaving the wind free to move underneath the floor and making it difficult to keep the schoolroom above warm. Uninsulated wood floors and single-paned windows were small deterrents for the winter's chill. The sour smell of stove oil smoke was familiar in most of our homes but here it seemed more noxious. Perhaps the tall evergreens surrounding the building served to capture the smoke and send it back to us.

While the older children listened to the younger ones take turns reading aloud, the teacher taught a unit in science or social studies to a class of combined grades of four and five or five and six. The following year a different unit would be taught to a similarly combined grouping until all of the required units in the curriculum were covered, with the detail and levels of expected understanding depending on the grade mix. The oldest students were called upon to take responsibility and assist wherever needed.

Pupils who demonstrated mastery of a topic were singled out to explain it to the others, and excellence was encouraged. For the most part, Grade 8 students worked independently. A similar system was the norm in one-room schools all across Canada and it appears such modest- costing methods of educating a population have served my age mates well.

Although it was only October, preparations for the Christmas Concert had begun in earnest, led by Mr. Hazzard. In Rock Bay, the Christmas Concert was the highlight of the first half of the school year. We called it a Christmas Concert too, with no thought that the faith of some members in our community, or even our teacher, might have been other than Christian. Of the twenty-eight children in our one-room school, at least two-thirds of them – the Jays – had parents of Chinese heritage and may well have had a different faith. Such issues never arose.

The concert itself was held in the logging company's dining hall, with a single dress rehearsal on the afternoon of the Saturday evening event. It was only after the camp had shut down for Christmas and the single men who lived in the bunkhouse and ate in the cookhouse had gone home that the space became available for use by the school.

For many weeks during the autumn, some part of our school day was devoted to preparing for it: singing, costuming, decorations and artwork. The wonderful display, however homespun, gave each child a visible part to play and became the spectacle that was our Christmas Concert. Mothers were called upon to supply or sew critical items for the Nativity Scene. During the afternoons, pupils practiced their roles at the back of the room, gathered around the oil stove that sputtered and belched smoke at the most inopportune times.

Finally the last week of school in 1948 had arrived, and the classroom buzzed with excitement. Mornings were devoted to only the most important subjects, what we now know as core curriculum. Our teacher had pretty well decided what he would write on each child's report card so he could allow us to put the finishing touches on plans for the concert. In one corner a student practiced his speaking lines with a classmate listening and correcting. Freddy Jay was practicing to be the Master of Ceremonies this year and his part included reciting 'Twas the Night before Christmas before the curtains opened to show our manger scene. The only Grade 1 girl in the school that year was to perform All I Want for Christmas Is My Two Front Teeth. We knew she was a good choice when we head her lisp out the words through the gaps in her teeth.

I had brought my sleeping-eyes doll from home to be the Baby Jesus this year. We had finally agreed which of the offered doll beds would be the cradle for my doll, and Carol was carefully draping it with a blanket she had borrowed from her mother.

We devoted time every afternoon to perfecting the carols we would sing on the big night. Mr. Hazard's ability at the keyboard was somewhat mediocre, but he picked out the tunes for us to follow along with our singing. Although I was aware I had never been able to carry a tune any more than my Dad could, I enjoyed the opportunity to sing those well-known Christmas carols.

If we were good, Mr. Hazzard might play for us to sing a few of the popular Christmas songs we didn't know as well, and wouldn't be called upon to sing as a group. Sometimes he played one of his personal records on the gramophone, like Burl Ives or Gene Autry, while we completed some art work or coloured pictures. And then the last Friday came. Once we were dismissed, we rushed home to brief our parents on what help was needed of them.

On Saturday morning the Dads pushed the long cookhouse tables against the walls and lined up the bench seats in rows facing the kitchen, which would serve as our dressing room. Under the direction of several moms, the same dads hung sheets on strong fishing line across the opening where the cooks ordinarily came and went to serve food. By the time we arrived for dress rehearsal, the space was transformed.

For all of us, Saturday night dinner was hurried, followed by a rush to be ready and in our places at the cookhouse before half-past six, for makeup and last minute instruction. Moms and dads sat on the benches, leaving enough room for their children to join them later. The little brothers and sisters preferred the space in front, on the plank floor, carefully swept with plank floor cleaning powder, Dustbane, after all the setting up had been finished.

At the sound of a tinkling bell backstage, the audience stopped talking and sat upright. Children on the floor were shushed; the concert began. Behind the curtain Freddy Jay, whom I secretly admired, read *The Night before Christmas* in his strong clear voice. Then, holding her by the hand, Fred escorted a grinning Penny, his cousin, through the curtains to her place in front of the audience. Her rendition of *All I Want for Christmas is My Two Front Teeth* was a delight, and brought down the house with applause. We were off to a good start.

Behind the curtains, we arranged and rearranged robes, wings, shepherds' staffs, and headgear. When big Bill Graham, who had no wife or children, shone his powerful flashlight from the back of the hall on to the wall above the curtain, it was time for the Nativity pageant to begin. Mr. Hazzard had selected the cast carefully so that every pupil in the school would be shown off to their best advantage. He wanted no one to be overlooked, and for each of his students to go home with parents proud of the role their child had played.

After the four Christmas carols we had practiced so diligently were performed, Freddy appealed to the audience to sing along with *Jingle Bells*, followed by *Have a Holly, Jolly Christmas*. Then he announced one more carol, *Silent Night*, for everyone's participation. With that last song the concert was over. Once the children came into the hall after casting off their costumes, it was evident by each parent's greetings that we had done well. There were hugs and laughter until a loud, "Ho, Ho, Ho, Merry Christmas!" coming from the door behind us interrupted the festivities. A fat Santa arrived, carrying a huge sack of gifts.

It was well known among the camp parents that Granite Bay Timber was generous in supplying a gift for each of the children in the community, both school-aged and not. Earlier that month, a small committee of parents--I know because my mother was one of them--had shopped for the gifts in Laver's Department Store in Campbell River, and the store had graciously gift-wrapped them. Each of us was called by Santa to receive our gift and, in addition, we each received a brown paper bag to take home, which contained a mandarin orange, candy cane and chocolate or other candy, together with another toy or small game.

After Santa's departure, both children and adults enjoyed their time together over hot chocolate or a cold drink, probably Kool Aid, with sandwiches and cookies made by the mothers. The evening complete, we walked home ready to begin an important holiday time at home with our families.

Any child in a family that celebrates Christmas finds anticipation of the big event almost impossible to bear. My sister Judy and I knew the time was getting close when Mom began to bake cookies. Shortbread was first because it kept the best; if Mom could hide it well enough, that is.

Dad used a lot of butter in his regular meals, which he slathered generously on some foods I thought were fine without it. It's not surprising then, that shortbread was my father's favourite cookie, and he ate more of it than anyone else. He was also an important participant in the making of it. Mom would put the butter out to warm from the heat of the kitchen in a large ceramic brown betty bowl. Then as soon as Dad was available, after work or on Sunday, she drafted him into service.

Mom explained that because Dad was so much stronger, he was more able to wield the wooden spoon she used to cream the sugar into the softened butter. She was adamant that lengthy careful mixing at this stage, which required patience and muscle power, was the secret of her melt-in the-mouth result. When my father had achieved the right consistency, mom added the other ingredients as he continued to stir. A vigorous working of the resulting mixture with his enormous hands was the last step before Mom formed the dough into cookie rolls. After the rolls of cookie dough had chilled in the outdoor cooler for a few hours or overnight, she cut them into slices for baking.

From snatches of women's conversations in Rock Bay, I discovered just how much the other women living in camp coveted my mother's shortbread cookies: first because they were so tender and tasty and second because she was able to enlist my father's help, while they were expected to complete the job alone. Dad took no other responsibility for food preparation, but apparently this important gesture set him apart from the other husbands. With the shortbread making completed, my sister and I could look forward to at least a week of cookie production, with a different tempting variety cooling on racks every day.

My mother was always generous about sharing the bounty from her kitchen. From her storehouse of Christmas baking she would arrange an assortment of cookies, tarts and Christmas cake on a plate covered with a tea towel, and send one of us out to deliver the treat.

Old Mr. Graney was one of the elderly folks: he lived in a tumbling-down wooden shack, just on the other side of the rickety footbridge over the creek. It was an adventure to visit him in his sparse home. I marvelled that anyone, even an elderly bachelor, could live in such disarray, wearing greasy clothing that actually smelled of crankcase oil.

There was also Mr. and Mrs. Johnson whose house was in a second tier of houses high on the hill above the creek mouth and its booms, with a panoramic ocean view beyond The Rock. The Johnsons were most appreciative of mom's gesture, and found ways of extending our visit with conversation over tea in their tidy home.

The two families who were our closest friends in camp received bigger parcels from my mother's kitchen. Mom packaged theirs in a chocolate box or biscuit tin lined with waxed paper, and delivered them herself in the afternoon while we were at school, or we took them as a family after supper in the evening. Mr. and Mrs. Bird, and their son, Bill, along with the Pinette family, with their three young children, all became our lifelong friends.

The Birds and Pinettes lived directly across from our home and just behind the log dump. Bill Bird Sr. drove a logging truck, and Romeo Pinette ran the dump machine, so they were entitled to live in camp houses.

Taking the Christmas offering to Old Teddy Hill was my favourite stop because he always had a chocolate bar for the kids when they came to the commissary. One of the most memorable characters in Rock Bay, Ted was the company timekeeper and first aid attendant. As the camp had a long history without fatalities, and only occasional cuts and scrapes to be bandaged, Teddy, as he was affectionately known, was alone for most of his day time. He opened the commissary every evening for a few hours after the crews came in, and after supper until most of the men had settled in the bunkhouse for the night. That still left him a lot of time alone with his ever-present bottle of hard liquor.

I rarely saw him absolutely sober. He was not ever really drunk but frequently seemed to lean a bit when he came to our house for a coffee or a game of cribbage. It was testament to my father's good humour that he suffered this lonely man to have access to our family. The only time I remember my father asking anyone to leave our home was one evening when Ted began to use bad language. Dad would not tolerate that because it wasn't fitting for women's ears. I heard later that poor old Ted came back the next day, when I was at school, to apologize to Mom for his excesses. In return she presented him with a warm loaf of bread fresh from the oven.

⚜

Secrets buzzed in our house as the days of December ticked along. Strangely-shaped parcels disguised in brown paper began to appear and almost as quickly to disappear. The used wrapping paper that Mom had saved from previous years began to disappear. The sticky tape, always in limited supply, was all used up.

Our celebration of Christmas day itself remained much as it had been when we lived on the float, except for the three missing family members, of course. It was our practice to visit Nano and Grandpa for a day just before or immediately after Christmas day when we were able to enjoy a meal with the traditional Norwegian specialties their home was known for. Of course Uncle Ingolf was available to join us that day too.

For me the holidays meant time to read, and also time to be with dad aboard *Lutie*, when he went out looking for good logs along the shore. He supplemented his earnings by beachcombing those logs that broke loose from booms in the worst winter storms, logs driven high on the beach by the wind and waves. December saw some of the highest tides of the year, making it easier then to hook on to them and pull them off. Beachcombing at this time of the year could prove fruitful when he pulled a lost log off the beach with *Lutie's* strong engine.

Now that Uncle Ingolf and Grandpa Andy had moved to Campbell River, dad was working alone on the hand logging claim. During the Christmas school holiday and the camp shutdown there were other ways, mostly in the outdoors, which Mom and Judy preferred to spend the short daylight hours of winter months. Snow meant snowball fights with the kids still in camp and, if there was enough on the ground, we could build a snow fort. Making a snowman was a given and mom helped by donating her scarf and dad's old fedora.

On the years when it was really cold, a shallow lake a few miles up the logging road froze so we could go skating. One of the dads went on ahead to confirm the ice was thick enough. Ice on the *bull pen,* where the logs were dropped, indicated there was a good chance the lake ice was safe. Then plans were made for a group to drive to the lake and enjoy an afternoon of skating.

Buster, Judy, Myrtle, Myrtle and Bill Bird with Bill Jr. crossing on the creek bridge.

Gunhild's Granddaughter

Dad and Bill Bird Sr. must have skated a lot in their childhood because I remember them as strong skaters. With great delight I found I could actually stand up on those narrow blades. Mom had borrowed her brother's skates, and although my ankles were not as strong as those of the more experienced skaters, my muscular thighs helped and I could do it, one of the few athletic activities I ever accomplished. After several fun times on the frozen lake, I asked for, and received, a pair of white figure skates for Christmas that year. Purchased large for my growing feet, those skates stayed with me for many, many years.

Really cold winters were uncommon in coastal communities and when they came we took measures to prevent our water pipes from freezing overnight, when there was no draw of water. The best method available was to leave the cold water tap running at night with just a light stream.

On Boxing Day one winter, mom and dad took Judy and me on the *Lutie* to the Elk Bay logging camp, where Dad's friend Martin was the watchman. Martin was spending the Christmas shutdown alone there. Mom had her usual package of baking for him and Dad thought the overnight outing would be a welcome change for Martin and for us.

Martin was a good cook and fed us well – a full turkey dinner. What I remember most was the fun we had exploring the big cookhouse with the huge pots and heavy dishes like they used at the Rock Bay camp, which we had never been allowed to explore. I noted the special way the cook, or a flunky usually, set the long tables covered with white oilcloth. Camp procedure was for the dinner plate to be laid down first, turned upside down to keep it free of dust I assumed. On it and also turned over, was a bowl for cereal or dessert, then an upright saucer with a cup, also upside down.

Returning home the next day, my parents were dismayed to find that although their carefully adjusted cold water flow had worked and was still running, the un-insulated sink drain under the house was exposed to wind and it had frozen. With nowhere to go, the running water had overflowed the sink. This flooded the tough and tested Battleship brand linoleum covering the kitchen floor and we arrived home to find an indoor skating rink of ice over most of the 800 square feet of our home.

Gunhild's Granddaughter

8.
High School – Grade 9

G oing to high school promised to be a scary new experience. Almost worse was the idea of living away from home for the first time. The dusty, bumpy trip by car from Rock Bay to Campbell River had been familiar but driving up to this hulking building, where I was to have my own room in Betty and Grant McMillan's home, made me feel uncomfortable. At home Judy and I shared a room with bunk beds. There was barely standing room in our tiny bedroom; the dresser drawers and desk were all built-in.

I was not aware that Betty and Grant MacMillan were family friends but Dad had known Grant, a truck driver, through logging. They wanted to make sure their seven-year old son travelled safely on the school bus, and after school I was to look after him. I supposed the babysitting was in exchange for my room and board.

How mom and dad had made the decision to send me away was a mystery at the time. Many years later my sister told me about their decision-making process. She said our parents agonized over it because the only alternative they had was for mom and Judy to move with me to Campbell River and establish another home there. That would have left dad in the Rock Bay house living on his own. When Judy was old enough for high school, four years later, they all resettled in Campbell River, by which time I was ready to move away again.

The MacMillan house was in Campbellton, set high on a hill at the north end of Peterson Road, well above and facing the Campbell River. The driveway to the house from the road wound between second growth cedar and fir. Only enough space for the house had been cleared of trees, and as we approached our car kicked up bark dust and dirt from the imperfectly bulldozed road. The outside of the house was without siding or plaster, only battens held the tarpaper in place.

As we stepped inside, we were met by a friendly couple who were obviously working hard to complete their massive project. While Dad and Grant talked about Grant's slow process of home building, Betty showed me to my room.

"We thought you would like to have this room, Myrtle. The bathroom is next to it right here, and we managed to get the door hung last weekend."

The whole house was divided by two-by-fours that showed edges of pink insulation stuffed between each eighteen-inch interval. The room she was showing me and the bathroom both had doors but other rooms in this big house shell did not.

"It's nice Betty. This will be the first time I've had my own room. Our house is really small by comparison."

The living area of their home seemed unnecessarily spacious—such a change from what I was used to. I supposed such a big home space would be hard to heat in winter, but there was a fireplace. Some of the tall evergreens appeared threatening, and blocked some of the light through my bedroom window. The windows of our little house in Rock Bay gave a full view of everything on all sides.

"I'll let you get settled here now. Billy is playing outside with the neighbour boys, but he'll be in for supper and you can meet him then."

My room was sparse. There was a single camp bed, a well-used dresser and an apparently homemade desk with a tired chrome kitchen chair. There seemed to be plenty of blankets on the bed, at least, and a crocheted, or maybe knitted, bedspread.

Having three drawers for my own use and a separate hanging cupboard for my meagre clothing was beyond imagining. Tomorrow was the first day of school, and I was feeling very unsure of myself.

When Dad called to say he was leaving, I came out to say goodbye. There wasn't much left to say for we had talked in the car on the way.

"I want to get ahead of the guys returning to camp from their weekend out," he said. "The Sunday traffic dust was bad enough coming here. Besides, the tide is good for booming at six tomorrow morning so it will be early to bed for me. I suppose you'll be doing that too, Myrtle." He gave me a hug and landed one of his familiar, slobbery kisses on my cheek.

We had talked or rather he had, as he drove along. It wasn't until we were on the outskirts of the community and were just crossing the bridge over the Campbell River that he had finally gathered the courage to broach an uncomfortable topic. "Your mother and I have brought you up to know right from wrong, so we expect you'll make the right decisions now you're on your own and away from home." I could tell he really wanted to say more but had decided to leave well enough alone once he had managed to get the main message out.

I was less than two months past my thirteenth birthday and more naive that even I realized, but my parents were letting me loose in the world. They were demonstrating their faith in my ability to cope, and I grabbed the opportunity to be on my own and ran with it. In fact, once away I didn't ever really feel a need, or desire, to go back.

On the Sunday evening a week later, I gathered together the pages for my big, new binder and arranged dividers for each of the different subjects: English, social studies, math, science, and home economics. I wouldn't need sections for PE or guidance. The morning bus trip to school was itself an adventure. As Billy and I stood waiting at the end of the long driveway before 7:30 AM, we could hear the bus coming as it rumbled up Peterson Hill. Together with the boys from the house across the street, we were the first ones on board. I came to know their family better when their mother asked me to baby-sit most Saturday evenings. In this newly-developed neighbourhood there were apparently few girls available to her, and having a suitably aged, proven-capable sitter living just across the street was a huge bonus. I welcomed the 25 cents an hour they paid— the going rate then—as it supplemented the $20 my parents gave me as a monthly allowance.

As the bus wound its way along Peterson Road through the farming community, it kicked up gravel and dust, and at each stop along the way picked up a smattering of children, none of whom appeared to be older than Grade 7. The chatter among them grew as their numbers increased and we neared the school. Eventually the bus pulled up in front of the little elementary school that served farm folks whose homes were situated across the wide, flat land behind the more populated Campbell River village centre.

Its elementary-school passengers disgorged, the bus continued, picking up occasional high school students before it began passing modest bungalows. It finally came onto a paved city street that led directly to Campbell River High School. There it pulled up under the overhanging roof that, on rainy days, became a play yard with paved surface. The clock on the stuccoed outside wall showed 8:05. Now what was I supposed to do?

That first hour wandering the halls of the school became the very worst part of my whole school day. It continued that way for the entire Grade 9 year and no matter what I thought to do there was no way to avoid the feeling of loneliness. When their bus arrived early, students who were athletic-minded gathered to play in the gym with other kids who were on sports teams and had come for a scheduled team practice. Art students could go to the art room as soon as the teacher arrived. Secretarial students could always go to the typing room and practice to improve their typing speed, Miss Tunningly came in early for them.

Other early arrivals all disappeared somewhere, leaving me to stroll the hallways until first bell when I could go to my homeroom where Mr. Monk, a senior English teacher, would be preparing lessons for the day. During later grades I learned some students—including those who walked to school—gathered in the "smoke pit" located behind the stage. That was never part of my world either.

Those first days were a blur of new ideas and procedures. I was confused by the need to move to a different room for each subject while the teachers remained in place to welcome the incoming class. Fortunately some of the teachers made a point of standing just outside their classroom so that people like me could ask their way to the next classroom on their schedule. After the first few weeks in this new world it all began to be more familiar.

Still, as my footsteps echoed back to me, I felt friend-less and unimportant, somehow out of place. At the end of the second floor hallway there was a large picture window that offered a full vista of the ocean and the rows of houses clus-tered along the street below me. Some mornings I stood there watching students climbing the steep hill to the school. Little did I know that two years later I would be struggling up that same hill myself every morning.

As the weeks wore on I discovered that Clara, who was in my classes, and her sister, Mary, lived in Campbellton too, on one of the flat streets just below Betty and Grant's home. They invited me to walk down on a Saturday so we could spend some time together. Both were serious students also, so it was nice to have someone to share homework problems with. Mary was an avid collector of movie magazines, which she shared with us, and, as we became better acquainted, walk-ing in to the village for a Saturday afternoon movie together became routine.

Later in the year, I became friends with Diana, who was in my home room. Through her I met the young people whom she had known since they started school together in Grade 1. Diana's father, Mr. Hudson, and Magistrate Roderick Haig-Brown, had emigrated from England about the same time, so their two families and all of the children were close. Diana's family owned a large property facing the mouth of the Campbell River and the Painter family (of Painter's Lodge) lived on the adjacent property. All of them accepted me as a newcomer, but one having a rural and water-wise upbringing similar to their own. They were all bound together by their same elementary school history and over time they learned about my early school experiences.

My early bus arrival still set me apart—none of my new friends came so early—leaving me to continue as a lost figure wandering every morning. I eventually realized the bus I took made a second run in the morning to pick up children from another area outside of town. The added disadvantage of my designated bus was that it left for the home trip immediately after the last class, allowing me no time to participate in after-school activities even if I had wanted to.

View of Discovery Passage and Cape Mudge on Quadra Island.

9.
High School – Grade 10

SEPTEMBER, 1952

This year would be different from the last. For one thing, I would not have to ride the school bus. Better still, on weekday mornings I could sleep a bit later since the school was only two long blocks away, and I could almost leave as late as when the first bell rang.

There were two other main differences. I would be sharing my bedroom with someone else, the way I did at home. Also like at home, this was a tiny two-bedroom house. Betty and Del Pelletier owned and operated the Variety Store downtown, and they worked long hours in it. They wanted me here to help keep track of their son, Richie, and sometimes play games with him or help with his homework. He seemed a good boy and appeared happy to take the top bunk, but maybe not so happy about going to bed before I did.

We had agreed that if his parents were out or had gone back to work after supper, I could listen to him read or help practice his spelling for the Friday tests. They explained that if it was busy in the store during the day, and they went back to unpack, price and restock the shelves as they often did, I was in charge. Any details pertaining to a financial exchange between my parents and my hosts I was never aware of, nor did I concern myself about. I was secure there, and when the house was quiet I could do my own homework, read or listen to their records. They had a tiny television too, my first exposure to the "box."

My homeroom this year was on the second floor. The room had a whole wall of windows facing Discovery Passage. Seeing the familiar ocean made me feel more comfortable in this classroom, even surrounded as it was by new-to-me scientific equipment. I could look as far south as Cape Mudge on Quadra Island and over the treetops to the north to the sulphurous smoke from the Crown Zellerbach pulp mill, when the wind blew toward the township. People on the street, coughing from the rotten-egg-gas commented it was the smell of money.

The mill manager's daughter was new this year, from the United States and in Grade 10 with me, but her homeroom was on the first floor and amid typewriters used by Miss Tunningly's secretarial pupils. Mr. Wittingham, my home room teacher, also taught me science. When I arrived at the classroom each day he was always ready to talk to us about 'big' world issues as he set out equipment and prepared for lessons he would be teaching that day. During the next year he was my chemistry teacher.

I liked living so close to the school and sometimes even walked along the edge of the playground back to the house to have my lunch. After school, there was no great hurry to be home as Rich had plenty of friends to play with on the way from his elementary school. Betty would sometimes phone and ask me to start dinner for them, but since otherwise my homework and monitoring Richie were my only responsibilities, it was a good place for me to be.

The store began to get really busy in early November that year, with new stock arriving every day, and I was delighted when Del asked me if I would like to help them out. Richie could come along with me and help under his parent's direction. Pricing new inventory as it arrived and stocking shelves with many new and some fascinating items was my first paying job, other than babysitting, and I recognized its importance. It was one more step toward independence.

As the days came closer to Christmas, Betty and Del taught me how to use the cash register and correctly count out change. That was new to me, too, but by following their careful teaching and with regular practice, I learned another valuable life skill. When my proficiency met their requirements, I was allowed to sell, take money and give change.

The Variety Store was always a Mecca for young people without much money who were shopping for gifts for their family and friends. They liked that I had a few ideas from my knowledge of the stock to help them decide what might be a good choice and meet their budget restrictions.

Mom and Dad always looked forward to having me at home again so they were disappointed when Betty and Del wanted me to work in the store until the day before Christmas. They picked me up at noon on Christmas Eve, and I went home with Christmas parcels that I had been able to buy with my own earned money. I even had enough left to buy a Kitten brand Orlon sweater for myself when they went on sale in January.

My grandmother Gunhild had become ill during the winter when I lived with the Pelletier's and died suddenly on July 1st, after I had gone home. Mom and dad had taken me back to Rock Bay to spend the summer, and having no further job prospects, certainly none there, I looked forward to a dreary time without friends or any excitement, for the remainder of the summer.

Visiting Grandpa Andy on White Rock beach.

The passing of White Nano seems unreal to me still – I remember few details. Little was said at the time, and I've come to realize my parents were protecting me from the loss, which of course was theirs too. It was the common practice then, to save children from the realities of dying, memorials, funerals, burials and all that went along with death. I understand it better now, since the same philosophy showed itself in my mother-in-law who was horrified years later to

Gunhild's Granddaughter

learn I had explained immediately to my young children that their paternal granddad was gone forever. Children were not expected to attend a funeral. I certainly don't remember being there when my grandparents were interred, but I have been to the gravesite where both White Nano and Grandpa Andy are buried.

With Nano gone, Grandpa Andy was inconsolable – he was eighty-two years old and never had been very good living alone. During the early years in the United States and Canada he had a partner to work with and share chores, since then Nano had been his rock. Having him stay alone in the Thulin Street house was impossible; fortunately his son, Ingolf, was near.

It then remained for my parents and my aunt and uncle to decide how my grandfather was to be looked after. Daughters seem to be the solvers of care problems – my Aunt Elsie undertook to find somewhere for Grandpa to live. She identified a pleasant retirement home close to her place on the mainland, in New Westminster. The home was in White Rock, not far from Vancouver and near the ocean. Mom and dad transported him there. I remember taking several trips with them and visiting Grandpa in White Rock where he lived comfortably, and apparently in his own world until his death in 1955.

I do remember a serious conversation I had with my parents after Nano died. They explained dad's parents had told each of their children never to expect either parent to live with them. To my grandparents, it was a matter of principal, and having set that standard, my sister and I were able to rest easy about our own decisions of having mom and dad in care. As it turned out, mom suffered a stroke that left her paralysed and without speech, thus requiring residential care. Dad stayed in the house alone for several months, with daily home care, but was relieved when we agreed to find him a senior's residence. He told us he was lonely without Hazel and wanted to move where he could have people around.

10.
High School – Grade 11

SEPTEMBER, 1953

This year I went to live with my uncle and his new wife, Helen. Helen and her sister had operated a successful, independent, seamstress business in a house they shared, also on Thulin Street. Ingolf had met them when he was building his house there.

Helen was a devout Roman Catholic and, because Ingolf was not, they were unable to be married in the main part of the big church that Helen attended regularly. An alcove to the side of the church building, much like a vestibule, was allocated for their nuptials. When my mom explained all this to me, I realized it was the first time I had been personally confronted by any issues of religious differences; among our people, a person's belief system was never discussed and certainly not argued.

Fortunately, the Forberg wedding guests were few in number, and since many members of Aunt Helen's huge family still lived in Quebec, there was room for everyone who came. At the wedding we met her two sisters and two brothers who lived in Campbell River. Her mother and father, parents of twelve children, had come all the way across the country from Gaspé to witness their daughter's marriage.

Mom had explained that my uncle had to promise Helen's priest that any children they had would be raised Catholic. Here again was new knowledge about the importance of religion to some people and the difficulties that could be encountered.

It was hard for me to grow accustomed to thinking of Dad's brother as a married man. Uncle Ingolf had been such an important and steady influence in my childhood on the floats, that the adjustment to his having someone sharing his life was especially difficult. She was nice though, and I liked her well enough.

When Dad and his brother had wound up Forberg Logging, Ingolf moved to Campbell River and took some time off to build a house of his own on the lot he had bought on Thulin Street. On a hill above and just one block behind the main street that ran along the oceanfront, it had a nice view of Discovery Passage, Quadra Island and the Cape Mudge lighthouse beyond.

I'm certain that view influenced both of these purchases by people whose whole lives had been spent on the ocean. Since the Forbergs moved to Thulin Street, the properties between theirs and the ocean were fully developed with residences and landscaping, so that if you go there now you would find no view of the ocean from houses on their side of the street.

At the beginning of the school year I had settled into their home, my new aunt big with child and my uncle working a job he had taken at the Crown Zellerback pulp mill, the major employer in the community. It was shift work, as were all positions there, and it turned out Ingolf hated the job, especially the revolving shift system. The advantage was it allowed him to be

Gunhild's Granddaughter

at home in Campbell River instead of away working for seven to ten days at a time, logging with my father. The household schedule was broken up with Ingolf's sleep and meal routine, then when Uncle Ingolf was a new dad, by baby Donald's waking and sleeping patterns, too.

Donald seemed to cry a lot – at least it was my impression when I was home. Mom said he had colic; fortunately I've never had any trouble sleeping so he did not keep me awake at night. Helen and Ingolf liked having me there to fill in holding the baby or staying home with him when Aunt Helen needed to go out. Knowing I could be a help to them must have been the reason my parents had arranged for me to live with them that year.

I enjoyed living there, as it was so close to downtown. Being able to walk everywhere I wanted to go, provided me even greater independence. I especially appreciated being able to walk the three short blocks to school, uphill as they were, leaving and returning home on my schedule. As I struggled upwards each morning, laden with binder and heavy text books on my hip, I was once more reminded of that lonely first year of wandering the halls early in the morning after the bus deposited me at school.

At the beginning of Grade 11, a new principal, Mr. Phillipson, arrived on the scene and he impressed me. What I most vividly remember was his opening address to the whole school at our first assembly that year. Unlike most high schools today, we were still small enough to all be assembled in the gymnasium, seated in the bleachers and chairs on the floor, to hear our new leader. What he told us about privileges and responsibilities seemed to make so much sense; to me it does still. His premise was that as we became older and rose through the grades at school, we would be given more choices, independence and freedom, but with that came an increasingly greater degree of responsibility. If we were not prepared to embrace the responsibility associated with a freedom or an independent choice, the privileges would be withdrawn until we learned the necessary responsibility lessons. He went on, years later, to become a superintendent of schools in another district; in my opinion he was certainly deserving of such promotion.

That year, Jeanne came into my life when she arrived part way through the year. She was my first real girlfriend; we were soul sisters, although the term wasn't known then, sharing many secrets and even double-dating during the short time she went to school in Campbell River. Jeanne lived with her aunt and uncle at the police station, just below the hill we lived on, so it was convenient for us to spend time together. Her uncle was the sergeant in charge of the Royal Canadian Mounted Police (RCMP) detachment in town, and his family accommodation was attached to the station. As her guardian, he was quite strict and gave her curfews that I was never subjected to. While boarding and making my own decisions, I was free to come and go, and I can't say I would have behaved differently had Uncle Ingolf placed time restrictions on me. I wasn't perfect; there were dances and parties, movies and fun times, but always in the back of my mind there was my father's admonition that I would act as my parents had taught and now expected of me.

An application I had made for work that summer at a local ladies' wear shop was successful so I was spared the need to return to Rock Bay for the whole summer holiday. I quickly made arrangements to stay with Grandpa Bill and Little Nano in their modest home under the hill at Willow Point. In a windowed space by the front door, there was a settee, a kind of day bed and that was my comfortable retreat. On my days off I participated in some of the crafts she was particularly talented with and helped in the garden as well. For me it was a good time to catch up on reading some of the thick books I had been saving for when there was no school homework.

View from the school bus to and from school in Grade 12.

11.
High School – Grade 12

I was back to riding a school bus this year, but the trip to school from my stop on the oceanside highway south of Willow Point didn't take nearly as long as the Peterson Road trip had. We left much later in the morning from Dahl Road and arrived just in time to get there before first bell. I recognized some of the students riding with me on this bus trip, since we were all going to the high school. The elementary students went on another bus, going in a different direction.

This year mom and dad had arranged for me to board with Gloria and Walter Sovde. Walter was a long-time logger friend of dad's, ten years younger than he, whose Swedish parents had been friends with dad's folks. Dad's friendship with Walter was apparently sealed when my teenaged father brought Oh Henry chocolate bars to young Walter, on his way home from boat outings with the older guys.

Although there were differences, and they argued passionately about their native countries, the up-coast Scandinavian families tended to support each other in friendly and thoughtful ways. What financial arrangements were made for my room and board I, again, never knew, but it was a comfortable existence for me. Their home was spacious and newly built, and my room pleasantly large and nicely furnished. I was once more within view of the ocean. What more could I ask?

Gloria and Walter had two little ones, David and Sandra, who only occasionally needed babysitting, because Gloria was a stay-at-home mom. In those days it was assumed any mother of young children would be at home, at least until the youngest was in school. The best part about being at the Sovde's home was that Gloria was a really good cook. She let me copy my personal favourites of her recipes, and sometimes, when the kitchen was free on the weekend, she let me practice. By that time, I was beginning to collect recipes to be used when I married, but as the year proceeded I became more convinced that my current boyfriend, who had begun to talk marriage, was pushing me into something I wasn't ready for. I broke off with him over it and was left to find a date for the all-important graduation dance that June. Fortunately there was a good supply of university students in the community, sent here for summer employment, (BC Telephone and the John Hart Dam for two examples) who wanted to be part of the social scene, and I lucked out.

I found there was a lot of homework in Grade 12 as a result of my heavily academic program, but my home economics classes continued to provide a needed respite. When I look back – on occasion I've been asked to recall my mentors' names – I immediately think of Mrs. Carpenter, who died a relatively young woman, and Miss Perkins, who I and my classmates living in the community know now as Francis Clive. To them I credit the idea of a career in Home Economics.

In the foods class I was encouraged to try new recipe combinations, and in the senior clothing class I created my graduation gown, a full skirted strapless bit of fluff made from taffeta and layers of white tulle. The previous year, I had sewed a flattering halter dress in a soft teal that served me well for some of the dances and parties.

Several other Campbell River High School teachers are memorable. For both years that I attended French classes, the same teacher was in charge, and his mannerisms resulted in my irrational dislike of the language. It seemed to us he was leering, perhaps even drooling, over the girls assigned to his class, making it difficult for us to attend to the lesson at hand. Better examples of memorable people were my English and Math teachers, Mr. Miles and Mr. Fogg respectively.

By this time I had gained some confidence within the student body and had accepted minor leadership positions that added to the culture of the school. I occasionally wrote bits for the student newspaper, and nearer the year's end, did some work on the student yearbook. It may have been here that I began to enjoy formatting and layout of photographs that I find so pleasurable to this day.

I've said our high school was relatively small -- approximately four hundred students if memory serves me well. In the academic stream of our graduating class there were only sixteen students, and a few more in the general program. One day in late May, a call came on the PA system, "Myrtle Forberg please report to the principal's office." You can imagine how that hit me. What had I ever done wrong? Was someone sick or hurt at home? Or … what?

On arriving at the office, I was met by Mr. Phillipson and ushered into his office where Mr. Fogg and Mr. Miles were sitting. The principal began by saying, "We've been reviewing your records and wondered if you had given any thought to going on to university?"

The Graduate's Grand March with Kernel Boogie
music was popular then.

Me, I thought? *Not a bit.* But I answered politely, "No, not really. No one in my family has had much education. I think my aunt might have finished Grade 12 but she was the only one." I continued, "She worked as a telephone operator to support herself in the city and married when she was much older."

They responded, "We have an application for scholarship here to have a chance for extra money to continue your education, and we thought you should fill it out."

Considering I had never contemplated university it seemed a strange request. I was barely calm enough to admit, "I could never afford to go to university."

Then Mr. Fogg added, "You know you'll have to write government final exams for all your academic courses anyway. The school isn't accredited yet."

I had written government finals the previous year for some Grade 11 courses, but hadn't given a thought to the reason for it. Still shaken by this unexpected meeting I asked, "What do they want to know?" I was concerned remembering an argument with my father who would never allow me to fill in the part of the counsellor's form where it asked for the parent's annual income. His secretive nature about the privacy of money issues was part of the reason why I never knew if, or how much, he paid for board so I could attend high school.

"We have already completed some parts of the form," was the reply. "Here they are, you just have to fill in the personal details and write a short essay about why you would like to have this scholarship to be a teacher," Mr. Phillipson told me.

To be a teacher was it? I thought. *Well that would be okay. Better than working in Pat's Style Shop where I would be this summer.* "Maybe you can write the essay on the weekend and bring it in to me on Monday morning," he continued. "Then I can get it mailed off for you next week."

And so I did, and the envelope went on its way.

During the spring, my mother and father had purchased a home on Hilchey Road and when the school year was over they moved from Rock Bay because Judy would be entering high school in September. If I had thought about it at the time, I could have felt slighted for having been boarded out while my sister got to live at home. The truth was I enjoyed the independence that living away allowed. It was assumed, of course, I would live there too, and I did, but it was only ever for the summer months. The home of my parents was my registered home address until I married six years later.

Myrtle dressed for work, 1955

Although my mother and sister settled in quickly – dad went back to work shifts in the bush or on the boom – I didn't ever feel at home in the Hilchey neighbourhood, nor did I know the neighbours, aside for some of their names. Of the other four places I had previously lived while attending high school, I felt no particular attachment to those either. The one exception was during Grade 11, at Uncle Ingolf's home, where through him and my aunt I had met some of their neighbours: Helen's sister and brother-in-law, who lived across the street and employed me as a baby-sitter; their boarder, Helen's brothers Max; Willie, who visited; Eric, the bachelor, who lived on the same street and, of course, Jeanne, was only a block away down the hill.

It was the summer of 1955 that I learned to drive. Dad had purchased a new Ford pickup at a discounted price, because it had ugly bumps and

Gunhild's Granddaughter

scrapes from being rolled in the ditch when it was still new, but he never had it repaired. It worked beautifully, but it was a stick-shift vehicle. Mom was a good teacher, insisting I learn to parallel park correctly. We took benefit of a quiet street on a Sunday afternoon, and as she instructed, I made the required moves.

"Now pull up close beside that car, put it in reverse, turn the steering wheel so your rear wheels nearly touch the curb, steer the other way now, continue backing up. There you've done it, pull ahead a bit closer in to the curb. Well done."

Soon I was using Dad's truck to go off to work at Pat's Style Shop in town each day, while Judy and mom chose furniture, arranged the house and prepared a real garden. The garden was mom's first love, and the lovely setting she created around the house seems to have survived. I've driven slowly by that house and there it is: the circle driveway, carport, and a slope-roofed addition at the back that became the spare room, all surrounded by perennials and annuals like the ones she chose.

It felt really strange to once again share a room with my sister – this room was small too – but even more unfamiliar was leaving from my parent's home for an evening out and being asked what time I would be home. Stranger yet was introducing my family to my date or to the young people picking me up. I'm sure my family experienced the same strangeness of having me there too.

Reflection:

I recently attended a high school reunion to commemorate 100 years of public schools in the Campbell River community. Everyone who had graduated, or been scheduled to graduate, from 1959 and before, was invited. Other reunions for my class have been held every decade or so but this was a much bigger event, celebrating the very first school to be established. A seafront hotel (then owned by the Thulin family, the grandparents of a former classmate) was used. One of the pupils of the first graduating class of Campbell River High School spoke to those assembled for the occasion and reviewed the various stages in development of a school system that had brought us through the years to the present Campbell River School District.

Several of the girls I chummed with had died, others had moved far enough away that travel costs to return for the celebration were prohibitive, but my one very close friend, Diana who still lives in town, was there. Several others, whom I remembered well, had helped on the planning committee. It was an opportune time for me to remember those high school years and speculate about the people who had been important to me then.

As each graduating year of former students came forward to have their group photographs taken, I was surprised by how few of them I knew. This was not a phenomenon of forgotten names – we were all wearing name tags – it was more a feeling of "was I even there?" The boys I found attractive then seemed weary and much diminished now, even the man whom, at one time, I had considered marrying. A few others carried on interesting conversations about where they had been and how their lives had developed. Although talking with them who seemed friendly was pleasant, they all seemed separated from me by my present life. Of all those people present, I had remained in contact with only one; that dear friend, Diana, whom I see annually, if that.

What I realized, in a flash of insight, was that my interests were so far removed from those of the more popular and thus recognizable school population, that my having been at the school just didn't seem to matter. Who mattered were the girls and boys on the basketball and volleyball teams, the cheerleaders, the student council members and the track team, all those students that at one time or other had worn the Carihi uniforms and represented their school in some public and photographable form.

Thinking further about this I also knew that the people who had remained in town, or who had returned after a time away, were the ones having the best time that evening. It felt uncomfortable to consider this and seemed more than a bit elitist, but I concluded they had never moved much beyond the small town they knew in high school. Does that make sense? It's the only way I can explain how I felt.

Crown Zellerbach owned Elk Falls Pulp and Paper Mill.

Afterward

The scholarship gave me entry into a new world of possibilities and I am forever thankful for that. Although I later learned the scholarship awarded to me had no other candidates, it was still mine, and I was determined to run with it. Without the scholarship my choices would have been to work in a menial job and then get married, with the expectation of babies to follow soon after. Up until the spring I had never even contemplated university.

Mom and dad had not considered university for me either. Dad had agreed it was probably a good idea for me to have something to fall back on. He meant if my husband died, or left me. Our family knew little of either experience. Now the choices were expanded, and though I still wasn't sure I wanted to be a teacher, this was the place I needed to start. And so I began.

SEPTEMBER, 1955

I'm standing with several hundred mostly young people, in a line that doesn't seem to be moving. This is the first day of registration for classes at University of British Columbia and thankfully it's restricted to first year students. Tomorrow, and for the rest of the week, all of the other students wanting to register will form one long queue. What must that be like? If I can finish the process today I won't have to find out.

In my hands are the papers that were mailed to me with instructions: "Bring these documents with you to complete the registration process." I'm still trying to make sense of the first-year student handbook that also came in the mail. Carefully secure in my purse is a document saying I am entitled to a $2,000 Crown Zellerbach Scholarship for each of the next five years, provided I maintain a necessary grade standard. The letter, on the company's official green-logo letterhead stationery, indicates the first year portion of the money will be deposited as soon as I am registered. I'm looking forward to seeing how this process unfolds - - - - -

To learn how Myrtle's career and life unfolded look for *Beyond the Floathouse, People and Places* available at the usual places.

About the Author

Myrtle Siebert.

Myrtle grew up in a floathouse in Port Neville inlet on the remote BC coast. All mail and supplies arrived every two weeks, via the Union Steamships, school was by correspondence, taught by mothers, transportation was by boat. At 9 years of age she entered a one-room school at Rock Bay, and then high school in Campbell River, where she was a boarder/babysitter in different homes each year.

She credits a high school principal, a very lucky break, and a 5-year industry scholarship, for opening the way to UBC enrollment, age 16. This logger's daughter found a career beyond the expected marriage and motherhood. Her home economics degree opened doors to a variety of careers: teacher, business owner, home builder and decorator, and now gardener, mother and grandmother.

Myrtle honed leadership skills through volunteering, begun within CFUW Nanaimo, and currently with CFUW Victoria and CFUW Saanich Peninsula. With so much gained from that one scholarship, we can understand her passion for volunteer fundraising in aid of higher education.

In 1992 she joined ITC, now POWER*talk* International, and has advanced in her membership up to level 4, Accomplished Communicator.

For more detail and purchasing information, please visit Myrtle's page at **http://www.myrtlesiebert.com**

Also by the Author

NON-FICTION

- **Management and Foods** (Out of Print).
- **Food for Life** (Out of Print).
- *from Fjord to Floathouse*, one family's journey from the farmlands of Norway to the coast of British Columbia – the story of a Norwegian immigrant couple over 100 years of family history.
- *Beyond the Floathouse*, Gunhild's Granddaughter – memoir.
- *Beyond the Floathouse*, People and Places – memoir coming in 2016.

WORKSHOPS

- Beginner Writing, Beginning your Family History, Remote BC Floathouse Life.